Java Functional Programming - Lambda & Stream

Practice Tests

By: Udayan Khattry

DEDICATION

This book is dedicated to my wife Neha, with love.

Copyright © 2021 Udayan Khattry
ISBN: 9781980718413
Imprint: Independently published

All rights reserved. No part of this book may be reproduced in any form or by any electronic or mechanical means, including information storage and retrieval systems, without permission in writing from the author.

01-Apr-2018:	v1.00 (1st Release)
04-Jan-2019:	v1.01
21-Aug-2019:	v1.02
10-Oct-2019:	v1.03
01-Nov-2021:	v1.04

Author's Profile

Udayan Khattry
SCJP, SCWCD & Oracle Database SQL Certified Expert

Author has a master's degree in Computer Applications from Symbiosis International University, Pune, India and have completed following professional certifications:
- **SCJP** 1.6 (Sun Certified Programmer for J2SE 6.0)
- **SCWCD** 1.5 (Sun Certified Web Component Developer)
- **Oracle Database SQL Certified Expert**

After working as a software developer and consultant for over 9 years for various companies in India, Dubai & Singapore, he decided to follow his lifelong passion of teaching.

In the last 5 years, author has published multiple books and online courses on Java and Java certifications. He currently has 67000+ students from 140+ countries.

Audience

Anyone who wants to assess their Java Functional Programming skills including : Lambda, Method Reference, Built-in Functional interfaces & Stream API.

Java Functional Programming - Lambda & Stream Practice Tests

Udemy Courses By Author

Course Link	**Java Certification (1Z0-819) Topic-wise Tests - Part 1** **535 multiple choice questions with explanation to assess Oracle Certified Professional, Java SE 11 Developer exam preparation** This course covers questions on following **5 exam topics:** - Working with Java data types - Controlling Program Flow - Java Object-Oriented Approach - Exception Handling - Working with Arrays and Collections
Course Link	https://www.udemy.com/course/ocp_java-se-11_1z0-819_p1/?referralCode=94723C1A0CB233CD799E
	Java Certification (1Z0-819) Topic-wise Tests - Part 2 **567 multiple choice questions with explanation to assess Oracle Certified Professional, Java SE 11 Developer exam preparation** This course covers questions on following **8 exam topics:** - Working with Streams and Lambda expressions - Java Platform Module System - Concurrency - Java I/O API - Secure Coding in Java SE Application - Database Applications with JDBC - Localization - Annotations
Course Link	https://www.udemy.com/course/ocp_java-se-11_1z0-819_p2/?referralCode=0E765C48B618E866CB79

Java Functional Programming - Lambda & Stream Practice Tests

	Java Certification (1Z0-819) Exam Simulation - Part 1 **Questions in these Practice tests** are randomized to give a real examination feel. All topics listed above are divided appropriately in **6 tests consisting of 300 questions in total.** Questions are designed based on real examination questions in terms of pattern and complexity. **All Exam topics and sub-topics are covered.**
Course Link	https://www.udemy.com/course/java-11_1z0-819_p1/?referralCode=360ED8841D658B856247
	Java Certification (1Z0-819) Exam Simulation - Part 2 **Questions in these Practice tests** are randomized to give a real examination feel. All topics listed above are divided appropriately in **6 tests consisting of 300 questions in total.** Questions are designed based on real examination questions in terms of pattern and complexity. **All Exam topics and sub-topics are covered.**
Course Link	https://www.udemy.com/course/java-11_1z0-819_p2/?referralCode=9A6070157511183345C8
	Java Certification (1Z0-819) Exam Simulation - Part 3 **Questions in these Practice tests** are randomized to give a real examination feel. All topics listed above are divided appropriately in **5 tests consisting of 251 questions in total.** Questions are designed based on real examination questions in terms of pattern and complexity. **All Exam topics and sub-topics are covered.**
Course Link	https://www.udemy.com/course/java-11_1z0-819_p3/?referralCode=019E14731CC414A03B1D

Java Functional Programming - Lambda & Stream Practice Tests

	Java Certification (1Z0-819) Exam Simulation - Part 4
	Questions in these Practice tests are randomized to give a real examination feel. All topics listed above are divided appropriately in **5 tests consisting of 251 questions in total.** Questions are designed based on real examination questions in terms of pattern and complexity. **All Exam topics and sub-topics are covered.**
Course Link	https://www.udemy.com/course/java-11_1z0-819_p4/?referralCode=0876CB0955C2942C81CF
	Java Certification (1Z0-815) Exam Simulation [2021]
	492 multiple choice questions with explanation to assess Oracle Certified Professional, Java SE 11 Programmer I exam preparation **Practice tests** are randomized to give a real examination feel. All topics listed above are divided appropriately in 6 **tests consisting of 82 questions each i.e., 492 questions in total.** Questions are designed based on real examination questions in terms of pattern and complexity. **All Exam topics and sub-topics are covered.**
Course Link	https://www.udemy.com/course/java-se-11_1z0-815/?referralCode=F409C96F9DD47698A3AE

Java Functional Programming - Lambda & Stream Practice Tests

	Java Certification (1Z0-815) Topic-wise Tests [2021]
	Multiple choice questions covering all the exam objectives of Java SE 11 Programmer I Exam **This course covers all the EXAM topics in orderly fashion, which will help students assess their preparation for respective topic.** This course can be used as a learning aid while preparing for 1Z0-815 certification to test your preparation for each topic while preparing for that topic.
Course Link	https://www.udemy.com/course/java-11_1z0-815/?referralCode=B0A027B28ACC27976961
	Java Certification : OCA (1Z0-808) Exam Simulation [2021]
	424 multiple choice questions with explanation to assess Oracle Certified Associate, Java SE 8 Programmer I preparation **Practice tests** are randomized to give a real examination feel. All topics listed above are divided appropriately in **4 tests consisting of 70 questions each i.e., 280 questions in total** and **2 bonus tests** containing **144 questions**. These questions are designed based on real examination questions in terms of pattern and complexity. **All Exam topics and sub-topics are covered.**
Course Link	https://www.udemy.com/course/java-oca/?referralCode=2337F77572B062EB41D6

Java Functional Programming - Lambda & Stream Practice Tests

	Java Certification - OCA (1Z0-808) Topic-wise Tests [2021] **Multiple choice questions covering all the exam objectives of Oracle Certified Associate, Java SE 8 Programmer I** This course covers **all the EXAM topics in orderly fashion,** which will help students assess their preparation for respective topic. Questions are designed based on real examination questions in terms of pattern and complexity. **All Exam topics and sub-topics are covered.**
Course Link	https://www.udemy.com/course/java-ocajp/?referralCode=AAD655BA1CE88EEE7DDC
	Java Certification : OCP (1Z0-809) Exam Simulation [2021] **540 multiple choice questions with explanation to assess Oracle Certified Professional, Java SE 8 Programmer II prep** **Practice tests** are randomized to give a real examination feel. All topics listed above are divided appropriately in **6 tests consisting of 90 questions each i.e., 540 questions in total.** Questions are designed based on real examination questions in terms of pattern and complexity. **All Exam topics and sub-topics are covered.**
Course Link	https://www.udemy.com/course/java-ocp/?referralCode=13982FCB1E0CAA5B94FB

Java Functional Programming - Lambda & Stream Practice Tests

	Java Certification - OCP (1Z0-809) Topic-wise Tests [2021] **Multiple choice questions covering all the exam objectives of Oracle Certified Professional, Java SE 8 Programmer II** This course covers **all the EXAM topics in orderly fashion**, which will help students assess their preparation for respective topic. Questions are designed based on real examination questions in terms of pattern and complexity. **All Exam topics and sub-topics are covered.**
Course Link	https://www.udemy.com/course/java-ocpjp/?referralCode=22BEEDC2D666C97BA703
	Test Java Functional Programming (Lambda & Stream) skills **180+ questions on Inner classes, Lambda expressions, Method References, Functional Interfaces & Stream API** **Practice tests** in this course will not only help you to assess your current knowledge of these topics but will also help you to revise the topics quickly. Questions are designed to *challenge your understanding of the topics*. Detailed explanations for all the questions are also provided for your reference.
Course Link	https://www.udemy.com/course/test-functional-programming/?referralCode=6A6A598EDD16CF40AA8E

Java Functional Programming - Lambda & Stream Practice Tests

	Java For Beginners - 1st step towards becoming a Java Guru! **Become a Java Expert with 22.5 hours of video content, 70+ coding challenges and 100+ Quiz questions** This course is for anyone who wants to learn Java from scratch, polish java skills, face java interviews and prepare for java certifications. Anyone can take this course and go from 0 developments skills to being expert in OOPs and core Java.
Course Link	https://www.udemy.com/course/corejava/?referralCode=831CD22E895230578AF2
	Python Quiz - Test your Python knowledge in 1 Day! **11th hour preparation for Python interviews, exams and tests with multiple choice questions** Basic to intermediate Python concepts are covered to assess your knowledge and skills. Questions are arranged in an orderly manner to provide ease of understanding.
Course Link	https://www.udemy.com/course/python-test/?referralCode=F070ABFC34905F36FF71

Java Functional Programming - Lambda & Stream Practice Tests

	Test your Core Java skills
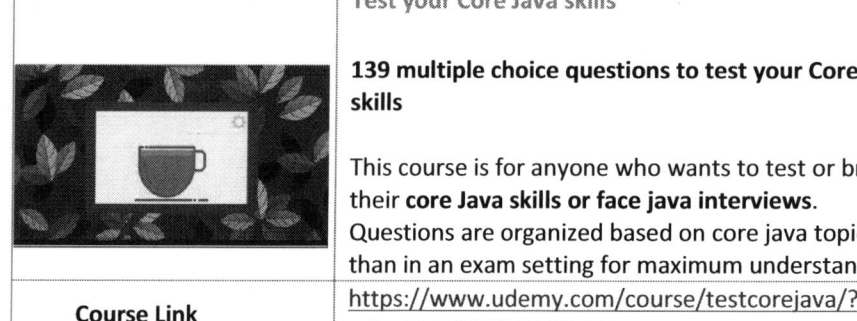	**139 multiple choice questions to test your Core Java skills** This course is for anyone who wants to test or brush up their **core Java skills or face java interviews**. Questions are organized based on core java topics rather than in an exam setting for maximum understanding.
Course Link	https://www.udemy.com/course/testcorejava/?referralCode=B8C939C8E3AEDA4EC4FD

NOTE: Please send an email to udayan.khattry@outlook.com to request for **MAXIMUM Discount coupon code (USD 9.99 or INR 360.00)** for above courses.

Java Functional Programming - Lambda & Stream Practice Tests

Table of Content

1	*Introduction*	*1*
2	*Assumptions*	*5*
1	*Practice Test-1*	*6*
2	*Practice Test-2*	*54*
3	*Practice Test-3*	*80*
4	*Practice Test-4*	*102*
5	*Practice Test-5*	*126*
6	*Practice Test-6*	*182*

1 Introduction

Learning is incomplete without challenging questions to assess the knowledge gained. There are courses and books available on Functional Programming & Stream API, which cover these topics in detail, but simply watching the video lectures or finishing the book will not give enough confidence unless the knowledge is validated.

Practice tests in this book will not only help you to assess your current knowledge of Java Functional Programming and Stream API but will also help you to revise the topics quickly. Questions are designed to challenge your understanding of the topics. Detailed explanations for all the questions are also provided for your reference.

Functional programming is not a new concept. Lambdas were implemented in other languages much before they were introduced in Java.

Before Java SE 8, anonymous inner classes with a single method was the closest Java came to functional programming but with lots of boilerplate code. If anyone wants to really appreciate the implementation of lambda expressions in java, it is necessary to know the anonymous inner classes in depth and to understand anonymous inner class you need to have knowledge of Regular and method-local inner classes.

You may face lots of questions in interviews or written tests where you are asked to convert anonymous inner class syntax to lambda expression and vice versa. Therefore I decided to start with questions on inner classes and then go on with Lambda expression, method references, built-in functional interfaces and finally end this test series with questions on Stream API.

All the questions in this book are validated against Java SE 8.

Java Functional Programming - Lambda & Stream Practice Tests

Following Topics are covered in this book:
1st practice test covers questions on:

- *Regular Inner class:*

  - Regular inner class and its syntax
  - Usage of this reference with Regular inner classes
  - Shadowing of Outer class variable by Inner class variable
  - Allowed access and non-access modifiers for Regular inner class
  - Accessing Regular inner class's name from within outer class and outside of outer class
  - Instantiating Regular inner class
  - Allowed and not allowed components inside a Regular inner class

- *Method-local inner class:*

  - Method-local inner class and its syntax
  - Modifiers used with method local inner classes
  - Relationship between method local inner class and top-level class
  - Where to create the instance of method local inner class?
  - Usage of local variables with method-local inner class

- *Anonymous inner class:*

  - Syntax of anonymous inner class
  - Inheritance and Polymorphism with anonymous inner class
  - Defining non-overriding methods in anonymous inner classes
  - Instance of anonymous inner class can be assigned to static variable, instance variable, local variable, method parameter and return value
  - Anonymous inner class extending from concrete class or abstract class or implementing an interface
  - Constructors and anonymous inner class

- *Static nested class:*

  - Syntax of static nested class
  - Accessing instance and static members of static nested class
  - Allowed access modifiers with static nested class
  - Nested interface defined within a class
  - Nested interface and nested class defined within an interface

2nd practice test will test, how well you know lambda expressions.

2nd Practice test covers questions on:

- Lambda expression and its syntax
- Arrow (->) operator
- Simplified Lambda expression syntax
- @FunctionalInterface annotation
- Requirements for an interface to be a Functional interface
- Convert anonymous inner class code to Lambda expression
- this within anonymous inner class vs this within lambda expression
- Usage of local variables with Lambda expression

Once you are comfortable with lambda expressions, then you can take 3rd practice test to assess your method references concepts.

3rd Practice test covers questions on:

- Method reference and its syntax
- Double colon (::) operator
- 4 types of method references:
    - Method Reference to Constructor
    - Method Reference to Static Method
    - Method reference to an Instance Method of a Particular Object
    - Method Reference to an Instance Method of an Arbitrary Object of a Particular Type
- Possibility of ambiguous call when a method reference syntax refers to both static and instance method of the class

Java 8 has provided various built-in functional interfaces, out of which 4 are most important and rest are dependent upon these 4 interfaces.

4th practice test covers questions on:

- Supplier interface
- Consumer interface and its default method: andThen
- Predicate interface and its default methods: and, or, negate
- Function interface and its default methods: compose, andThen
- Comparator interface, its static method: comparing and default methods: thenComparing, reversed

Java Functional Programming - Lambda & Stream Practice Tests

Stream API made the life of Java developers a lot easier.

5th practice test covers questions on:

- *Generic Stream interface and its primitive counterparts*
- *Creating sequential streams*
- *Important methods of Stream interface*
- *Generic Optional class and its primitive counterparts*
- *Convert arrays and collections to streams*
- *Sort a collection using Stream API*

After Stream support in Collection API, processing collection elements became a lot easier. Parallel streams can run tasks in parallel without writing cumbersome logic.

6th practice test covers questions on:

- *Method stream() of Collection interface*
- *Save results to a collection using the collect method and group/partition data using the Collectors class*
- *forEach(Consumer) method of Iterator<T> interface*
- *Convert arrays and collections to streams*
- *stream() and parallelStream() methods of Collection interface*
- *parallel() and sequential() method of Stream interface*
- *Behavior of various methods such as forEach, reduce, forEachOrdered, findFirst with parallel streams*

For any questions / queries / suggestions, please send an email to: udayan.khattry@outlook.com.

2 Assumptions

Questions mentioning line numbers: Because of wrapping one statement can be shown in multiple lines. If a question mentions line number, then consider the starting of line from the java statement / block perspective. In below code fragment, Line 14 represents 'catch(IllegalArgumentException | RuntimeException | Exception e) {' and not '| Exception e) {'.

There is no confusion for Line 15, it represents 'System.out.println(e.getMessage());' and Line 16 represents just the closing bracket, '}'

```java
public static void main(String [] args) {
    try {
        convert("");
    }
    catch(IllegalArgumentException | RuntimeException
        | Exception e) { //Line 14
        System.out.println(e.getMessage()); //Line 15
    } //Line 16
    catch(Exception e) {
        e.printStackTrace();
    }
}
```

1 Practice Test-1

1.1 This practice test covers questions on:

Regular Inner class:
- Regular inner class and its syntax
- Usage of this reference with Regular inner classes
- Shadowing of Outer class variable by Inner class variable
- Allowed access and non-access modifiers for Regular inner class
- Accessing Regular inner class's name from within outer class and outside of outer class
- Instantiating Regular inner class
- Allowed and not allowed components inside a Regular inner class

Method-local inner class:
- Method-local inner class and its syntax
- Modifiers used with method local inner classes
- Relationship between method local inner class and top-level class
- Where to create the instance of method local inner class?
- Usage of local variables with method-local inner class

Anonymous inner class:
- Syntax of anonymous inner class
- Inheritance and Polymorphism with anonymous inner class
- Defining non-overriding methods in anonymous inner classes
- Instance of anonymous inner class can be assigned to static variable, instance variable, local variable, method parameter and return value
- Anonymous inner class extending from concrete class or abstract class or implementing an interface
- Constructors and anonymous inner class

Static nested class:
- Syntax of static nested class
- Accessing instance and static members of static nested class
- Allowed access modifiers with static nested class
- Nested interface defined within a class
- Nested interface and nested class defined within an interface

1.1.1 Which of the following Inner class definition inserted in the Outer class, will print Udayan in the output on executing Test class?

```java
package com.udayan.innerclass;

class Outer {
    private String name = "Udayan";
    //Insert inner class definition here
}

public class Test {
    public static void main(String [] args) {
        new Outer().new Inner().printName();
    }
}
```

A.	```class Inner {` ` public void printName() {` ` System.out.println(this.name);` ` }` `}```
B.	```class Inner {` ` public void printName() {` ` System.out.println(name);` ` }` `}```
C.	```inner class Inner {` ` public void printName() {` ` System.out.println(name);` ` }` `}```
D.	```abstract class Inner {` ` public void printName() {` ` System.out.println(name);` ` }` `}```

1.1.2 Which of the following access modifiers can be used with regular inner classes? Select ALL that apply.

A. public
B. protected
C. default (don't specify anything)
D. private

1.1.3 Which statement when inserted in the main(String []) method will print "INNER" in the output? Select ALL that apply.

```java
package com.udayan.innerclass;

public class Test {
    class A {
        void m() {
            System.out.println("INNER");
        }
    }

    public static void main(String [] args) {
        //Insert statement here
    }
}
```

A.	`A a1 = new Test().new A();` `a1.m();`
B.	`Test.A a2 = new Test().new A();` `a2.m();`
C.	`A a3 = this.new A();` `a3.m();`
D.	`Test.A a4 = this.new A();` `a4.m();`

1.1.4 Which statement when inserted in the main(String []) method will print "Hello" in the output?

```java
package com.udayan.innerclass;

class A {
    private String str = "Hello";
    public class B {
        public B(String s) {
            if(s != null)
                str = s;
        }
        public void m1() {
            System.out.println(str);
        }
    }
}

public class Test {
    public static void main(String[] args) {
        //Insert statement here
    }
}
```

A.	new A().new B().m1();
B.	new A.B().m1();
C.	new A().new B("hello").m1();
D.	new A().new B(null).m1();

1.1.5 Which statement when inserted in the main(String []) method will print "WELCOME!" in the output?

```java
package com.udayan.innerclass;

class Outer {
    class Inner {
        public void m() {
            System.out.println("WELCOME!");
        }
    }
}
public class Test {
    public static void main(String[] args) {
        //Insert statement here
    }
}
```

A.	`Outer.Inner obj1 = new Outer().new Inner();` `obj1.m();`
B.	`Inner obj2 = new Outer().new Inner();` `obj2.m();`
C.	`Outer.Inner obj3 = this.new Inner();` `obj3.m();`
D.	`Inner obj4 = this.new Inner();` `obj4.m();`

1.1.6 Which of the following combinations of access modifiers can be used with top level classes?

A. public or protected

B. public or default (don't specify anything)

C. private or default (don't specify anything)

D. private or protected

1.1.7 What will be the result of compiling and executing Test class?

```java
package com.udayan.innerclass;

class A {
    A() {
        System.out.print(1);
    }
    class B {
        B() {
            System.out.print(2);
        }
    }
}

public class Test {
    public static void main(String [] args) {
        B obj = new A().new B();
    }
}
```

A. 12

B. 21

C. 2

D. Compilation error

1.1.8 What will be the result of compiling and executing Test class?

```java
package com.udayan.innerclass;

class Foo {
    public static void m1() {
        System.out.println("Foo : m1()");
    }
    class Bar {
        public static void m1() {
            System.out.println("Bar : m1()");
        }
    }
}

public class Test {
    public static void main(String [] args) {
        Foo foo = new Foo();
        Foo.Bar bar = foo.new Bar();
        bar.m1();
    }
}
```

A. Foo : m1()

B. Bar : m1()

C. Compilation error

D. Runtime exception

1.1.9 What will be the result of compiling and executing class M?

```java
package com.udayan.innerclass;

class M {
    private int num1 = 100;
    class N {
        private int num2 = 200;
    }

    public static void main(String[] args) {
        M outer = new M();
        M.N inner = outer.new N();
        System.out.println(outer.num1 + inner.num2);
    }
}
```

A. Compilation error

B. 300

C. 100

D. 200

1.1.10 What will be the result of compiling and executing class Test?

```java
package com.udayan.innerclass;

class X {
    class Y {
        private void m() {
            System.out.println("INNER");
        }
    }

    public void invokeInner() {
        Y obj = new Y(); //Line 9
        obj.m(); //Line 10
    }
}

public class Test {
    public static void main(String[] args) {
        new X().invokeInner();
    }
}
```

A. INNER

B. Compilation error at Line 9 as instance of outer class (X) is needed to create the instance of inner class (Y).

C. Compilation error at Line 10 as private method m() cannot be invoked outside the body of inner class (Y).

D. Exception is thrown at runtime.

1.1.11 What will be the result of compiling and executing the Test class?

```java
package com.udayan.innerclass;

class P {
    private int var = 100;
    class Q {
        String var = "Udayan";
        void print() {
            System.out.println(var);
        }
    }
}

public class Test {
    public static void main(String[] args) {
        new P().new Q().print();
    }
}
```

A. Udayan

B. 100

C. Compilation error

D. Exception is thrown at runtime

1.1.12 What will be the result of compiling and executing Test class?

```java
package com.udayan.innerclass;

class Foo {
    static { //static initialization block
        System.out.print(1);
    }
    class Bar {
        static { //static initialization block
            System.out.print(2);
        }
    }
}

public class Test {
    public static void main(String [] args) {
        new Foo().new Bar();
    }
}
```

A. 12

B. 21

C. Compilation error

D. Exception is thrown at runtime

1.1.13 Given code of Test.java file:

```java
package com.udayan.innerclass;

class Outer {
    Outer() {
        System.out.print(2);
    }
    /*INSERT 1*/

    class Inner {
        Inner() {
            System.out.print(4);
        }
        /*INSERT 2*/
    }
}

public class Test {
    public static void main(String[] args) {
        new Outer().new Inner();
    }
}
```

Currently on executing Test class, 24 is printed in the output.
Which of the following pairs will correctly replace /*INSERT 1*/ and /*INSERT 2*/ so that on executing Test class, 1234 is printed in the output?
Select ALL that apply.

A.	Replace /*INSERT 1*/ with {System.out.print(1);} Replace /*INSERT 2*/ with {System.out.print(3);}
B.	Replace /*INSERT 1*/ with static {System.out.print(1);} Replace /*INSERT 2*/ with {System.out.print(3);}
C.	Replace /*INSERT 1*/ with {System.out.print(1);} Replace /*INSERT 2*/ with static {System.out.print(3);}
D.	Replace /*INSERT 1*/ with static {System.out.print(1);} Replace /*INSERT 2*/ with static {System.out.print(3);}

1.1.14 What will be the result of compiling and executing Test class?

```java
package com.udayan.innerclass;

class Outer {
    public void print(int x) {
        class Inner {
            public void getX() {
                System.out.println(++x);
            }
        }
        Inner inner = new Inner();
        inner.getX();
    }
}

public class Test {
    public static void main(String[] args) {
        new Outer().print(100);
    }
}
```

A. 100

B. 101

C. Compilation error

D. Runtime exception

1.1.15 Which of the following options can replace /*INSERT*/ such that on executing Test class, "Hello World!" is displayed in the output?
Select ALL that apply.

```
package com.udayan.innerclass;

class A {
    public void someMethod(final String name) {
        /*INSERT*/ {
            void print() {
                System.out.println("Hello " + name);
            }
        }
        new B().print();
    }
}

public class Test {
    public static void main(String[] args) {
        new A().someMethod("World!");
    }
}
```

A. `public class B`

B. `protected class B`

C. `class B`

D. `private class B`

E. `final class B`

F. `abstract class B`

1.1.16 Which of the following options can replace /*INSERT*/ such that on executing TestOuter class, "HELLO" is printed in the output?
Select ALL that apply.

```java
package com.udayan.innerclass;

class Outer {
    public static void sayHello() {}
    static {
        class Inner {
            /*INSERT*/
        }
        new Inner();
    }
}

public class TestOuter {
    public static void main(String[] args) {
        Outer.sayHello();
    }
}
```

A.	`{`
	`    System.out.println("HELLO");`
	`}`

B.	`static {`
	`    System.out.println("HELLO");`
	`}`

C.	`Inner() {`
	`    System.out.println("HELLO");`
	`}`

D.	`Inner(String s) {`
	`    System.out.println(s);`
	`}`

1.1.17 What will be the result of compiling and executing Test class?

```java
package com.udayan.innerclass;

class A {
    public void print(String name) {
        class B {
            B() {
                System.out.println(name); //Line 5
            }
        }
    }
    B obj = new B(); //Line 9
}

public class Test {
    public static void main(String[] args) {
        new A().print("Udayan"); //Line 14
    }
}
```

A. Udayan

B. Compilation error at Line 5

C. Compilation error at Line 9

D. Compilation error at Line 14

1.1.18 What will be the result of compiling and executing Test class?

```java
package com.udayan.innerclass;

class Outer {
    private String msg = "A";
    public void print() {
        final String msg = "B";
        class Inner {
            public void print() {
                System.out.println(this.msg);
            }
        }
        Inner obj = new Inner();
        obj.print();
    }
}

public class Test {
    public static void main(String[] args) {
        new Outer().print();
    }
}
```

A. Compilation error

B. A

C. B

D. Exception is thrown at runtime

1.1.19 What will be the result of compiling and executing Test class?

```java
package com.udayan.innerclass;

class Message {
    public void printMessage() {
        System.out.println("Hello!");
    }
}

public class Test {
    public static void main(String[] args) {
        Message msg = new Message() {}; //Line 9
        msg.printMessage(); //Line 10
    }
}
```

A. Compilation error at Line 9

B. NullPointerException is thrown by Line 10

C. Hello!

D. HELLO!

1.1.20 What will be the result of compiling and executing Test class?

```java
package com.udayan.innerclass;

class Message {
    public void printMessage() {
        System.out.println("Hello!");
    }
}

public class Test {
    public static void main(String[] args) {
        Message msg = new Message() {
            public void PrintMessage() {
                System.out.println("HELLO!");
            }
        };
        msg.printMessage();
    }
}
```

A. Compilation error
B. Runtime error
C. Hello!
D. HELLO!

1.1.21 What will be the result of compiling and executing Test class?

```java
package com.udayan.innerclass;

class Message {
    public void printMessage() {
        System.out.println("Hello!");
    }
}

public class Test {
    public static void main(String[] args) {
        Message msg = new Message() {
            public void PrintMessage() {
                System.out.println("HELLO!");
            }
        };
        msg.PrintMessage();
    }
}
```

A. Compilation error
B. Runtime error
C. Hello!
D. HELLO!

1.1.22 What will be the result of compiling and executing Test class?

```java
class Message {
    public void printMessage() {
        System.out.println("Hello!");
    }
}

public class Test {
    public static void main(String[] args) {
        Message msg = new Message() {
            @Override
            public void PrintMessage() {
                System.out.println("HELLO!");
            }
        };
        msg.printMessage();
    }
}
```

A. Compilation error

B. Runtime error

C. Hello!

D. HELLO!

1.1.23 What will be the result of compiling and executing Test class?

```java
package com.udayan.innerclass;

abstract class Greetings {
    abstract void greet();
}

public class Test {
    public static void main(String[] args) {
        Greetings obj = new Greetings() {
            @Override
            public void greet() {
                System.out.println("Hello");
            }
        };
        obj.greet();
    }
}
```

A. Compilation error

B. NullPointerException

C. Hello

D. Nothing is printed on to the console

1.1.24 Which of the following options can replace /*INSERT*/ such that there are no compilation errors?

```java
package com.udayan.innerclass;

interface Flyable {
    void fly();
}

public class Test {
    public static void main(String[] args) {
        /*INSERT*/
    }
}
```

| A. | `Flyable flyable = new Flyable();` |
| B. | `Flyable flyable = new Flyable(){};` |
| C. | ```
Flyable flyable = new Flyable() {
    public void fly() {
        System.out.println("Flying high");
    }
}
``` |
| D. | ```
Flyable flyable = new Flyable() {
    public void fly() {
        System.out.println("Flying high");
    }
};
``` |

1.1.25 What will be the result of compiling and executing Test class?

```java
package com.udayan.innerclass;

interface I1 {
    void m1();
}

public class Test {
    public static void main(String[] args) {
        I1 i1 = new I1() {
            @Override
            public void m1() {
                System.out.println(1234);
            }
        }
        i1.m1();
    }
}
```

A. 1234

B. No output

C. Compilation error

D. Runtime exception

1.1.26 What will be the result of compiling and executing Test class?

```java
package com.udayan.innerclass;

public class Test {
    public static void main(String [] args) {
        System.out.println(new Object() {
            public String toString() {
                return "Anonymous";
            }
        });
    }
}
```

Which of the following is the correct way to make the variable 'passportNo' read only for any other class?

A. Anonymous

B. Some text containing @ symbol

C. Compilation error

D. Runtime exception

1.1.27 Which of the following options can replace /*INSERT*/ such that there are no compilation errors? Select ALL that apply.

```
package com.udayan.innerclass;

interface Sellable {
    double getPrice();
}

public class TestSellable {
    private static void printPrice(Sellable sellable) {
        System.out.println(sellable.getPrice());
    }

    public static void main(String[] args) {
        /*INSERT*/
    }
}
```

A.	`printPrice(null);`
B.	`printPrice(new Sellable());`
C.	`printPrice(new Sellable() {  });`

D.	`printPrice(new Sellable() {`
	`    @Override`
	`    public double getPrice() {`
	`        return 45.34;`
	`    }`
	`});`

1.1.28 What will be the result of compiling and executing TestPoint class?

```java
package com.udayan.innerclass;

import java.util.ArrayList;
import java.util.Collections;
import java.util.Comparator;
import java.util.List;

class Point {
    private int x;
    private int y;

    public Point(int x, int y) {
        this.x = x;
        this.y = y;
    }

    @Override
    public String toString() {
        return "Point(" + x + ", " + y + ")";
    }
}

public class TestPoint {
    public static void main(String [] args) {
        List<Point> points = new ArrayList<>();
        points.add(new Point(4, 5));
        points.add(new Point(6, 7));
        points.add(new Point(2, 2));

        Collections.sort(points, new Comparator<Point>() {
            @Override
            public int compare(Point o1, Point o2) {
                return o1.x - o2.x;
            }
        });
    }
}
```

A. [Point(2, 2), Point(4, 5), Point(6, 7)]

B. [Point(6, 7), Point(4, 5), Point(2, 2)]

C. [Point(4, 5), Point(6, 7), Point(2, 2)]

D. Compilation error

1.1.29 What will be the result of compiling and executing Test class?

```java
package com.udayan.innerclass;
import java.util.ArrayList;
import java.util.Collections;
import java.util.Comparator;
import java.util.List;

class Point {
    private int x;
    private int y;

    public Point(int x, int y) {
        this.x = x;
        this.y = y;
    }

    public int getX() {
        return x;
    }

    public int getY() {
        return y;
    }

    @Override
    public String toString() {
        return "Point(" + x + ", " + y + ")";
    }
}
public class Test {
    public static void main(String [] args) {
        List<Point> points = new ArrayList<>();
        points.add(new Point(4, 5));
        points.add(new Point(6, 7));
        points.add(new Point(2, 2));

        Collections.sort(points, new Comparator<Point>() {
            public int compareTo(Point o1, Point o2) {
```

```
                return o1.getX() - o2.getX();
            }
        });

        System.out.println(points);
    }
}
```

A. [Point(2, 2), Point(4, 5), Point(6, 7)]
B. [Point(6, 7), Point(4, 5), Point(2, 2)]
C. [Point(4, 5), Point(6, 7), Point(2, 2)]
D. Compilation error.

1.1.30 What will be the result of compiling and executing Test class?

```
package com.udayan.innerclass;

import java.util.ArrayList;
import java.util.Collections;
import java.util.Comparator;
import java.util.List;

class Point {
    private int x;
    private int y;

    public Point(int x, int y) {
        this.x = x;
        this.y = y;
    }

    public int getX() {
        return x;
    }

    public int getY() {
        return y;
    }

    @Override
    public String toString() {
        return "Point(" + x + ", " + y + ")";
```

```java
        }
}

public class Test {
    public static void main(String [] args) {
        List<Point> points = new ArrayList<>();
        points.add(new Point(4, 5));
        points.add(new Point(6, 7));
        points.add(new Point(2, 2));

        Collections.sort(points, new Comparator<Point>() {
            public int compare(Point o1, Point o2) {
                return o2.getX() - o1.getX();
            }
        });

        System.out.println(points);
    }
}
```

A. [Point(2, 2), Point(4, 5), Point(6, 7)]

B. [Point(6, 7), Point(4, 5), Point(2, 2)]

C. [Point(4, 5), Point(6, 7), Point(2, 2)]

D. Compilation error

1.1.31 Consider below code:

```java
package com.udayan.innerclass;

import java.util.Arrays;
import java.util.Collections;
import java.util.Comparator;
import java.util.List;

public class Test {
    public static void main(String [] args) {
        List<String> names =
            Arrays.asList("James", "diana", "Anna");

        /*INSERT*/

        System.out.println(names);
    }
}
```

Currently on executing Test class, [James, diana, Anna] is printed in the output.

Which of the following options can replace /*INSERT*/ such that on executing Test class, [Anna, diana, James] is printed in the output?

A.	`Collections.sort(names, new Comparator<String>() {`
	`    public int compare(String o1, String o2) {`
	`        return o1.compareTo(o2);`
	`    }`
	`});`

B.	`Collections.sort(names, new Comparator<String>() {`
	`    public int compare(String o1, String o2) {`
	`        return o1.compareToIgnoreCase(o2);`
	`    }`
	`});`

C.	`Collections.sort(names, new Comparator<String>() {`
	`    public int compare(String o1, String o2) {`
	`        return o2.compareTo(o1);`
	`    }`
	`});`

D.	`Collections.sort(names);`

1.1.32 Can an anonymous inner class implement multiple interfaces?

A. Yes
B. No

1.1.33 What will be the result of compiling and executing Test class?

```java
package com.udayan.innerclass;

enum ShapeType {
    CIRCLE, SQUARE, RECTANGLE;
}

abstract class Shape {
    private ShapeType type
            = ShapeType.SQUARE; //default ShapeType

    Shape(ShapeType type) {
        this.type = type;
    }

    public ShapeType getType() {
        return type;
    }

    abstract void draw();
}

public class Test {
    public static void main(String[] args) {
        Shape shape = new Shape() {
            @Override
            void draw() {
                System.out.println(
                    "Drawing a " + getType());
            }
        };
        shape.draw();
    }
}
```

A. Drawing a CIRCLE
B. Drawing a SQUARE
C. Drawing a RECTANGLE
D. Compilation error

1.1.34 Which of the following options can replace /*INSERT*/ such that there are no compilation errors?

```
package com.udayan.innerclass;

class A {
    static class B {

    }
}
public class Test {
    /*INSERT*/
}
```

A. B obj = new B();
B. B obj = new A.B();
C. A.B obj = new A.B();
D. A.B obj = new A().new B();

1.1.35 Which of the following options can replace /*INSERT*/ such that there on executing class A, output is: static nested class? Select ALL that apply.

```java
package com.udayan.innerclass;

public class A {
    private static class B {
        private void log() {
            System.out.println("static nested class");
        }
    }

    public static void main(String[] args) {
        /*INSERT*/
    }
}
```

A.	`B obj1 = new B();` `obj1.log();`
B.	`B obj3 = new A().new B();` `obj3.log();`
C.	`A.B obj2 = new A.B();` `obj2.log();`
D.	`A.B obj4 = new A().new B();` `obj4.log();`

1.1.36 What will be the result of compiling and executing Test class?

```java
package com.udayan.innerclass;

class Outer {
    abstract static class Animal { //Line 2
        abstract void eat();
    }

    static class Dog extends Animal { //Line 6
        void eat() { //Line 7
            System.out.println("Dog eats biscuits");
        }
    }
}

public class Test {
    public static void main(String[] args) {
        Outer.Animal animal = new Outer.Dog(); //Line 15
        animal.eat();
    }
}
```

A. Compilation error at Line 2

B. Compilation error at Line 6

C. Compilation error at Line 7

D. Compilation error at Line 15

E. Dog eats biscuits

1.1.37 What will be the result of compiling and executing Test class?

```java
package com.udayan.innerclass;

class Outer {
    private static int i = 10;
    private int j = 20;

    static class Inner {
        void add() {
            System.out.println(i + j);
        }
    }
}

public class Test {
    public static void main(String[] args) {
        Outer.Inner inner = new Outer.Inner();
        inner.add();
    }
}
```

A. Compilation error in Test class code

B. Compilation error in Inner class code

C. 30

D. Exception is thrown at runtime

1.1.38 Which of the following 2 options can replace /*INSERT*/ such that on executing class Test, output is: HELLO!? Select ALL that apply.

```java
package com.udayan.innerclass;

class Outer {
    static class Inner {
        static void greetings(String s) {
            System.out.println(s);
        }
    }
}

public class Test {
    public static void main(String[] args) {
        /*INSERT*/
    }
}
```

A.	`Outer.Inner inner1 = new Outer().new Inner();` `inner1.greetings("HELLO!");`
B.	`Outer.Inner inner2 = new Outer.Inner();` `inner2.greetings("HELLO!");`
C.	`Outer.Inner.greetings("HELLO!");`
D.	`Inner.greetings("HELLO!");`

Java Functional Programming - Lambda & Stream Practice Tests

1.1.39 Will below code compile successfully?

```
package com.udayan.innerclass;

class Outer {
    interface I1 {
        void m1();
    }
}
```

A. Yes

B. No

1.1.40 Will below code compile successfully?

```
package com.udayan.innerclass;

interface I1 {
    void m1();

    interface I2 {
        void m2();
    }

    abstract class A1 {
        public abstract void m3();
    }

    class A2 {
        public void m4() {
            System.out.println(4);
        }
    }
}
```

A. Yes

B. No

1.2 Answers of Practice Test - 1 with Explanation

1.1.1 Answer: B

Reason:
name can be referred either by name or Outer.this.name. There is no keyword with the name "inner" in java. As new Inner() is used in main method, hence cannot declare class Inner as abstract in this case. But note abstract or final can also be used with regular inner classes.
Keyword "this" inside Inner class refers to currently executing instance of Inner class and not the Outer class.
To access Outer class variable from within inner class you can use these 2 statements:
System.out.println(name); OR System.out.println(Outer.this.name);

1.1.2 Answer: A, B, C, D

Reason:
All four access modifiers (public, protected, default and private) and two non-access modifiers(final and abstract) can be used with Regular inner classes.

1.1.3 Answer: A, B

Reason:
There are 2 parts: 1st one is referring the name of inner class, A and 2nd one is creating the instance of inner class, A.
Now main method is inside Test class only, so inner class can be referred by 2 ways: A or Test.A.
As, A is Regular inner class, so instance of outer class is needed for creating the instance of inner class. As keyword "this" is not allowed inside main method, so instance of outer class, Test can only be obtained by new Test() as . Instance of inner class can be created by: new Test().new A();

Java Functional Programming - Lambda & Stream Practice Tests

1.1.4   Answer: D

Reason:
new B() will cause compilation error as no-argument constructor is not defined in inner class B. new A.B() is invalid syntax for creating the instance of Regular inner classes. new A().new B("hello").m1(); is a valid syntax but it will print "hello" in the output and not "Hello".

1.1.5   Answer: A

Reason:
There are 2 parts: 1st one is referring the name of inner class, Inner and 2nd one is creating an instance of inner class, Inner.
Now main method is outside Outer class only, so inner class can be referred by one way only and that is by using outer class name: Outer.Inner.
As, Inner is Regular inner class, so instance of outer class is needed for creating the instance of inner class. Instance of outer class, Outer can only be obtained by new Outer(). So, instance of inner class can be created by: new Outer().new Inner();
Also note, keyword "this" is not allowed static main method.

1.1.6   Answer: B

Reason:
Top level class can be specified with either public or default access modifiers.

1.1.7   Answer: D

Reason:
To refer to inner class name from outside the top level class, use the syntax: OUTER_CLASS.INNER_CLASS.
In this case, correct syntax to refer B from Test class is: A.B and not B.

1.1.8   Answer: C

Reason:
Regular inner class Bar cannot define any static methods. Method m1() is static and hence compilation error.

NOTE: Regular inner class cannot define anything static, except static final variables.

1.1.9   Answer: B

Reason:
Outer class (M) code has access to all the members of inner class (N) including private members, hence inner.num2 doesn't cause any compilation error.

1.1.10   Answer: A

Reason:
invokeInner() is instance method of outer class, X. So, implicit "this" reference is available for this method. this reference refers to the currently executing instance of outer class, X. So Java compiler converts Y obj = new Y(); to Y obj = this.new Y(); and hence this syntax has no issues. So Line 9 is fine.
Because of the special relationship between Outer and inner class, Outer and Inner class can very easily access each other's private members. Hence, no issues with Line 10 as well.
Given code compiles and executes fine and prints INNER to the console.

1.1.11   Answer: A

Reason:
In this example, inner class's variable var shadows the outer class's variable var. So output is Udayan.
Few points to note here: 1. If inner class shadows the variable of outer class, then Java compiler prepends "this." to the variable. System.out.println(var); is replaced by System.out.println(this.var);
2. If inner class does not shadow the variable of outer class, then Java compiler prepends "<outer_class>.this." to the variable. So, if class Q doesn't override the variable of class P, then System.out.println(var); is replaced by System.out.println(P.this.var);

In the given example, if you provide System.out.println(P.this.var); inside print() method, then output would be 100.

1.1.12   Answer: C

Reason:

Regular inner class cannot define anything static, except static final variables. In this case, static initialization block inside inner class Bar is not allowed.

1.1.13 Answer: A, B

Reason:
Regular inner class cannot define anything static, except static final variables. So static {System.out.print(3);} will cause compilation error.

If a class contains, constructor, instance initialization block and static initialization block and constructor is invoked, then the execution order is:
static initialization block, instance initialization block and then constructor.

1.1.14 Answer: C

Reason:
class Inner is method local inner class and it is accessing parameter variable x.
Starting with JDK 8, a method local inner class can access local variables and parameters of the enclosing block that are final or effectively final.
But the statement System.out.println(++x); tries to increment the value of variable x and hence compilation error.

1.1.15 Answer: C, E

Reason:
Method-local inner classes cannot be defined using explicit access modifiers (public, protected and private) but non-access modifiers: final and abstract can be used with method-local inner class. In this case, abstract is also not possible as new B() is used.

1.1.16 Answer: A, C

Reason:
static initialization block defined inside Outer class is invoked when static method sayHello is invoked.

Method-local inner class can be defined inside methods(static and non-static) and initialization blocks(static and non-static).

But like Regular inner class, method-local inner class cannot define anything static, except static final variables.

new Inner(); invokes the no-argument constructor of Inner class. So, System.out.println("HELLO") can either be provided inside no-argument constructor or instance initialization block.

1.1.17 Answer: C

Reason:
Instance of method-local inner class can only be created within the boundary of enclosing initialization block or enclosing method. B obj = new B(); is written outside the closing curly bracket of print(String) method and hence Line 9 causes compilation error. Starting with JDK 8, a method local inner class can access local variables and parameters of the enclosing block that are final or effectively final so no issues with Line 5.

1.1.18 Answer: A

Reason:
Keyword "this" inside method-local inner class refers to the instance of inner class. In this case this.msg refers to msg variable defined inside Inner class but there is no msg variable inside Inner class. Hence, this.msg causes compilation error. System.out.println(msg); will print B (msg shadows Outer class variable) and System.out.println(Outer.this.msg); will print A.

1.1.19 Answer: C

Reason:
Message msg = new Message() {}; means msg doesn't refer to an instance of Message class but to an instance of un-named sub class of Message class, which means to an instance of anonymous inner class. In this case, anonymous inner class code doesn't override printMessage() method of super class, Message. So at runtime, msg.printMessage() method invokes the printMessage() method defined in super class (Message) and Hello! is printed to the console.

1.1.20 Answer: C

Reason:
It is a valid anonymous inner class syntax. But anonymous inner class code doesn't override printMessage() method of Message class rather it defines a new method PrintMessage (P in upper case). Anonymous inner class allows to define methods not available in its super class, in this case PrintMessage() method.
But msg.printMessage(); statement invokes the printMessage method of super class, Message and thus "Hello!" gets printed in the output.

1.1.21 Answer: A

Reason:
Even though anonymous inner class allows to define methods not available in its super class but these methods cannot be invoked from outside the anonymous inner class code. Reason is very simple, methods are invoked on super class reference variable (msg) which is of Message type. And class Message is aware of the methods declared or defined within its boundary, printMessage() method in this case. So using Message class reference variable, methods defined in sub class cannot be invoked. So, msg.PrintMessage(); statement causes compilation error.

1.1.22 Answer: A

Reason:
@Override annotation is used for overriding method. But PrintMessage (P in upper case) method of anonymous inner class does not override printMessage (p in lower case) method of its super class, Message. Hence, @Override annotation causes compilation error.

1.1.23 Answer: C

Reason:
obj refers to an anonymous inner class instance extending from Greetings class and the anonymous inner class code correctly overrides greet() method. Code executes and prints Hello on to the console.

1.1.24 Answer: D

Reason:
new Flyable(); => Can't instantiate an interface.
new Flyable(){}; => fly() method is not implemented.
new Flyable() { public void fly() { System.out.println("Flying high"); } } => semicolon missing at the end
new Flyable() { public void fly() { System.out.println("Flying high"); } }; => correct syntax

1.1.25 Answer: C

Reason:
Semicolon is missing just before the statement i1.m1(); Wrong syntax of anonymous inner class.

1.1.26 Answer: A

Reason:
System.out.println(new Object()); invokes the toString() method defined in Object class, which prints fully qualified class name, @ symbol and hexadecimal value of hash code [Similar to java.lang.Object@15db9742]
In the given code, an instance of anonymous class extending Object class is passed to System.out.println() method and the anonymous class overrides the toString() method. Thus, at runtime overriding method is invoked, which prints "Anonymous" to the console.

1.1.27 Answer: A, D

Reason:
Instance of anonymous inner class can be assigned to static variable, instance variable, local variable, method parameter and return value. In this question, anonymous inner class instance is assigned to method parameter.

printPrice(null); => No compilation error as asked in the question but it throws NullPointerException,
printPrice(new Sellable()); => Cannot create an instance of Sellable type,
printPrice(new Sellable() {}); => getPrice() method is not implemented.

1.1.28   Answer: D

Reason:
x and y are private variables and are accessible within the boundary of Point class. TestPoint class is outside the boundary of Point class and hence o1.x and o2.x cause compilation error. Make sure to check the accessibility before working with the logic.

1.1.29   Answer: D

Reason:
Comparator interface has compare(...) method and not compareTo(...) method. Anonymous inner class's syntax doesn't implement compare(...) method and thus compilation error. Make sure to check the accessibility and interface method details before working with the logic.

1.1.30   Answer: B

Reason:
return o2.getX() - o1.getX(); means the Comparator is sorting the Point objects on descending value of x of Point objects.
To sort the Point objects in ascending order of x, use: return o1.getX() - o2.getX();
To sort the Point objects in ascending order of y, use: return o1.getY() - o2.getY();
To sort the Point objects in descending order of y, use: return o2.getY() - o1.getY();

1.1.31   Answer: B

Reason:
If you sort String in ascending order, then upper case letters appear before the lower case letters. So in this case if I sort the list in ascending order then the output will be [Anna, James, diana] and this is what Collections.sort(names); and o1.compareTo(o2); method calls do.
o2.compareTo(o1); sorts the same list in descending order: [diana, James, Anna] but you have to sort the list such that [Anna, diana, James] is printed in the output, which means sort the names in ascending order but in case-insensitive manner. String class has compareToIgnoreCase() method for such purpose.

1.1.32 Answer: B

Reason:
Unlike other inner classes, an anonymous inner class can either extend from one class or can implement one interface. It cannot extend and implement at the same time and it cannot implement multiple interfaces.

1.1.33 Answer: D

Reason:
At the time of creating the instance of anonymous inner class, new Shape() is used, which means it is looking for a no-argument constructor in anonymous inner class code, which would invoke the no-argument constructor of super class, Shape. But as parameterized constructor is specified in Shape class, so no-argument constructor is not provided by the compiler and hence compilation error.
To correct the compilation error pass the enum constant while instantiating anonymous inner class.
Shape shape = new Shape(ShapeType.CIRCLE) {...}; or you can even pass null: Shape shape = new Shape(null) {...}; OR provide the no-argument constructor in the Shape class: Shape(){}

1.1.34 Answer: C

Reason:
In this case, you have to write code outside class A. B is a static nested class and outside class A it is referred by A.B.
Instance of class B can be created by new A.B();

1.1.35 Answer: A, C

Reason:
static nested class can use all 4 access modifiers (public, protected, default and private) and 2 non-access modifiers (final and abstract).
static nested class can contain all type of members, static as well as non-static. This behavior is different from other inner classes as other inner classes don't allow to define anything static, except static final variables. This is the reason static nested class is not considered as inner class.

There are 2 parts in accessing static nested class: 1st one to access the static nested class's name and 2nd one to instantiate the static nested class.
Within the top-level class, a static nested class can be referred by 2 ways: TOP-LEVEL-CLASS.STATIC-NESTED-CLASS and STATIC-NESTED-CLASS. In this case, either use A.B or simply use B. Now for instantiating the static nested class, an instance of enclosing class cannot be used, which means in this case, I can't write new A().new B(). Correct way to instance static nested class is: new A.B(); but as main method is inside class A, hence I can even write new B(); as well.

Top-level class can easily access private members of inner or static nested class, so no issues in invoking log() method from within the definition of class A.

1.1.36 Answer: E

Reason:
A class can have multiple static nested classes. static nested class can use all 4 access modifiers (public, protected, default and private) and 2 non-access modifiers (final and abstract). No issues at Line 2. static nested class can extend from a class and can implement multiple interfaces so Line 6 compiles fine. No overriding rules were broken while overriding eat() method, so no issues at Line 7.

Test class is outside the boundary of class Outer. So Animal can be referred by Outer.Animal and Dog can be referred by Outer.Dog. Polymorphism is working in this case, super class (Outer.Animal) reference variable is referring to the instance of sub class (Outer.Dog). So, no issues at Line 15 as well.

Test class compiles and executes successfully and prints "Dog eats biscuits" in the console.

1.1.37 Answer: B

Reason:
static nested class cannot access non-static member of the Outer class using static reference. Hence usage of variable j in Inner class causes compilation error.

1.1.38 Answer: B, C

Reason:

Outside of top-level class, Outer, static nested class can be referred by using TOP-LEVEL-CLASS.STATIC-NESTED-CLASS. So, in this case correct way to refer static nested class is Outer.Inner. greetings(String) is a static method, so it can be invoked by using the class name, which is by the statement: Outer.Inner.greetings("...");

Even though it is not preferred to invoke static method in non-static manner, but you can use the instance of class to invoke its static method.

To Create the instance of static nested class, syntax is: new TOP-LEVEL-CLASS.STATIC-NESTED-CLASS(...);

in this case, new Outer.Inner();

1.1.39 Answer: A

Reason:

interface can be nested inside a class. Class Outer is top-level class and interface I1 is implicitly static.

Static nested interface can use all 4 access modifiers(public, protected, default and private).

1.1.40 Answer: A

Reason:

interface I2 is implicitly public and static (Nested interface). class A1 is implicitly public and static (Nested class). class A2 is implicitly public and static (Nested class). You cannot explicitly specify protected, default and private for nested classes and nested interfaces inside an interface.

2 Practice Test-2

2.1 This practice test covers questions on:

- Lambda expression and its syntax
- Arrow (->) operator
- Simplified Lambda expression syntax
- @FunctionalInterface annotation
- Requirements for an interface to be a Functional interface
- Convert anonymous inner class code to Lambda expression
- this within anonymous inner class vs this within lambda expression
- Usage of local variables with Lambda expression

Java Functional Programming - Lambda & Stream Practice Tests

2.1.1   Which of the following operator is used in lambda expressions?

   A. =>
   B. = >
   C. ->
   D. - >

2.1.2   For the given code:

```java
package com.udayan.lambda;

interface Printable {
    void print(String msg);
}

public class Test {
    public static void main(String[] args) {
        Printable obj = new Printable() {
            public void print(String msg) {
                System.out.println(msg);
            }
        };
        obj.print("Welcome!");
    }
}
```

Which of the following options successfully replace anonymous inner class code with lambda expression code?
Select ALL that apply.

A.	`Printable obj = (String msg) -> {System.out.println(msg);};`
B.	`Printable obj = (msg) -> {System.out.println(msg);};`
C.	`Printable obj = (msg) -> System.out.println(msg);`
D.	`Printable obj = msg -> System.out.println(msg);`
E.	`Printable obj = x -> System.out.println(x);`
F.	`Printable obj = y - > System.out.println(y);`

2.1.3   For the given code:

```java
package com.udayan.lambda;

interface Operator {
    int operate(int i, int j);
}

public class Test {
    public static void main(String[] args) {
        Operator opr = new Operator() {
            public int operate(int i, int j) {
                return i + j;
            }
        };
        System.out.println(opr.operate(10, 20));
    }
}
```

Which of the following options successfully replace anonymous inner class code with lambda expression code?

Select ALL that apply.

A.	`Operator opr = (int x, int y) -> { return x + y; };`
B.	`Operator opr = (x, y) -> { return x + y; };`
C.	`Operator opr = (x, y) -> return x + y;`
D.	`Operator opr = (x, y) -> x + y;`
E.	`Operator opr = x, y -> x + y;`

2.1.4 For the given code:

```java
package com.udayan.lambda;

abstract class Greetings {
    abstract void greet(String s);
}

public class Test {
    public static void main(String[] args) {
        Greetings obj = new Greetings() {
            public void greet(String s) {
                System.out.println(s);
            }
        };
        obj.greet("Happy New Year!");
    }
}
```

Which of the following options successfully replace anonymous inner class code with lambda expression code?

A.	`Greetings obj = (String s) -> {System.out.println(s.toUpperCase());};`
B.	`Greetings obj = s -> {System.out.println(s.toUpperCase());};`
C.	`Greetings obj = s -> System.out.println(s.toUpperCase());`
D.	Lambda expression cannot be used in this case

2.1.5   What is the purpose of below lambda expression?

```
(x, y) -> x + y;
```

A. It accepts two int arguments, adds them and returns the int value
B. It accepts two String arguments, concatenates them and returns the String instance
C. It accepts a String and an int arguments, concatenates them and returns the String instance
D. Not possible to define the purpose.

2.1.6   Which of the annotation is used for Functional Interface?

A. @Functional
B. @FI
C. @FunctionalInterface
D. @Functional Interface

2.1.7   Does below code compile successfully?

```
package com.udayan.lambda;

@FunctionalInterface
interface I1 {
    void print();
    boolean equals();
}
```

A. Yes

B. No

2.1.8 What will be the result of compiling and executing Test class?

```java
package com.udayan.lambda;

@FunctionalInterface
interface I4 {
    void print();
    boolean equals(Object obj);
}

public class Test {
    public static void main(String[] args) {
        I4 obj = () ->
            System.out.println("Lambda expression");
        obj.print();
    }
}
```

A. Compilation error

B. Lambda expression

C. No output

D. Runtime error

2.1.9 What will be the result of compiling and executing Test class?

```java
package com.udayan.lambda;

interface I1 {
    void print();
}

public class Test {
    public static void main(String[] args) {
        I1 obj = () -> System.out.println("Hello");
    }
}
```

A. Compilation error
B. Hello
C. Program compiles and executes successfully but nothing is printed on to the console
D. Runtime error

2.1.10 Consider below interface:

```
interface I2 {
    int calc(int x);
}
```

Which of the following is the correct lambda expression for I2?

A. `I2 obj1 = x -> return x*x;`
B. `I2 obj2 = (x) -> return x*x;`
C. `I2 obj3 = x - > x*x;`
D. `I2 obj4 = x -> x*x;`

2.1.11 Is below functional interface correctly defined?

```
package com.udayan.lambda;

@FunctionalInterface
interface I8 {
    boolean equals(Object obj);
}
```

A. Yes
B. No

2.1.12 What will be the result of compiling and executing Test class?

```java
package com.udayan.lambda;

@FunctionalInterface
interface I5 {
    void print();
}

public class Test {
    int i = 100;

    I5 obj1 = new I5() {
        int i = 200;
        public void print() {
            System.out.println(this.i);
        }
    };

    I5 obj2 = () -> {
        int i = 300;
        System.out.println(this.i);
    };

    public static void main(String[] args) {
        Test ques = new Test();
        ques.obj1.print();
        ques.obj2.print();
    }
}
```

A.	100 100	B.	200 300
C.	200 100	D.	100 300

2.1.13 What will be the result of compiling and executing Test class?

```java
package com.udayan.lambda;

@FunctionalInterface
interface I7 {
    void print();
}

public class Test {
    String var = "Lambda";
    class Inner {
        int var = 1000;
        I7 obj = () -> System.out.println(this.var);
    }

    public static void main(String[] args) {
        Inner inner = new Test().new Inner();
        inner.obj.print();
    }
}
```

A. Lambda

B. 1000

C. Compilation Error

D. None of the above

2.1.14 What will be the result of compiling and executing Test class?

```java
package com.udayan.lambda;

interface I9 {
    void print();
}

public class Test {
    public static void main(String[] args) {
        int i = 400;
        I9 obj = () -> System.out.println(i);
        obj.print();
        System.out.println(++i);
    }
}
```

A.	400 400	B.	400 401
C.	Compilation error	D.	Exception is thrown at runtime

2.1.15 What will be the result of compiling and executing Test class?

```java
package com.udayan.lambda;

interface I6 {
    void m6();
}

public class Test {
    public static void main(String[] args) {
        I6 obj = () -> {
            int i = 10;
            i++;
            System.out.println(i);
        };
        obj.m6();
    }
}
```

A. Compilation error
B. 10
C. 11
D. Exception is thrown at runtime

2.1.16 Which of the following code replaces the anonymous inner class code with lambda expression?

```java
package com.udayan.lambda;

interface I10 {
    void m(String s);
}

public class Test {
    public static void main(String[] args) {
        method(new I10() {
            @Override
            public void m(String s) {
                System.out.println(s.toUpperCase());
            }
        }, "good morning!");
    }

    private static void method(I10 obj, String text) {
        obj.m(text);
    }
}
```

A.	`method(s -> { System.out.println(s.toUpperCase()) }, "good morning!");`
B.	`method(s -> System.out.println(s.toUpperCase()), "good morning!");`
C.	`method(s -> s.toUpperCase(), "good morning!");`
D.	`method(s -> System.out.println(s.toUpperCase()));`

2.1.17 What will be the result of compiling and executing Test class?

```java
package com.udayan.lambda;

interface Formatter {
    public abstract String format(String s1, String s2);
}

public class Test {
    public static void main(String[] args) {
        Formatter f1 = (str1, str2) ->
                            str1 + "_" + str2.toUpperCase();
        System.out.println(f1.format("Udayan", "Khattry"));
    }
}
```

A. Udayan_Khattry

B. UDAYAN_Khattry

C. Udayan_KHATTRY

D. UDAYAN_KHATTRY

2.1.18 What will be the result of compiling and executing Test class?

```java
package com.udayan.lambda;

interface Operator<T> {
    public abstract T operation(T t1, T t2);
}

public class Test {
    public static void main(String[] args) {
        Operator<String> opr1 = (s1, s2) -> s1 + s2;
        Operator<Integer> opr2 = (i1, i2) -> i1 + i2;
        opr1.operation("Hello", "World");
        opr2.operation(10, 40);
    }
}
```

A.	Compilation error
B.	HelloWorld 50
C.	Program compiles and executes successfully but nothing is printed on to the console
D.	HelloWorld 1040

2.1.19 For the given code:

```java
package com.udayan.lambda;

interface Operator<T> {
    public abstract T operation(T t1, T t2);
}

public class Test {
    public static void main(String[] args) {
        System.out.println(new Operator<String>() {
            public String operation(String s1, String s2) {
                return s1 + s2;
            }
        });
    }
}
```

Which of the following options successfully replace anonymous inner class code with lambda expression code?

A.	`System.out.println((String s1, String s2) -> s1 + s2);`
B.	`System.out.println((s1, s2) -> s1 + s2);`
C.	`System.out.println((s1, s2) -> { return s1 + s2; });`
D.	None of the other options

2.1.20 Which of the following are Functional Interface in JDK 8? Select ALL that apply.

A. `java.util.Comparator`
B. `java.lang.Runnable`
C. `java.awt.event.ActionListener`
D. `java.io.Serializable`
E. `java.lang.Cloneable`

2.1.21 Consider below code:

```java
package com.udayan.lambda;

import java.util.Arrays;
import java.util.Collections;
import java.util.List;

class Name {
    String first;
    String last;

    public Name(String first, String last) {
        this.first = first;
        this.last = last;
    }

    public String getFirst() {
        return first;
    }

    public String getLast() {
        return last;
    }

    public String toString() {
        return first + " " + last;
    }

}

public class Test {
    public static void main(String[] args) {
        List<Name> names = Arrays.asList(
                        new Name("Peter", "Lee"),
                        new Name("John", "Smith"),
                        new Name("bonita", "smith"));

        /*INSERT*/

        System.out.println(names);
    }
}
```

Currently on executing Test class, [Peter Lee, John Smith, bonita smith] is displayed in the output.

Which of the following options can replace /*INSERT*/ such that on executing Test class, [bonita smith, John Smith, Peter Lee] is displayed in the output? The names list must be sorted in ascending order of first name in case-insensitive manner.
Select ALL that apply.

A.	`Collections.sort(names, (o1, o2) -> o1.getFirst()` `    .compareTo(o2.getFirst()));`

B.	`Collections.sort(names, (o1, o2) ->`
	`o1.getFirst().toLowerCase()`
	`    .compareTo(o2.getFirst().toLowerCase()));`

C.	`Collections.sort(names, (o1, o2) ->`
	`o1.getFirst().toUpperCase()`
	`    .compareTo(o2.getFirst().toUpperCase()));`

D.	`Collections.sort(names, (o1, o2) -> o1.getFirst()` `    .compareToIgnoreCase(o2.getFirst()));`

2.1.22 For the given code:

```java
package com.udayan.lambda;

interface Formatter<T> {
    T format(T t);
}

public class Test {
    public static void main(String[] args) {
        System.out.println(
            formatString("hello", /*INSERT*/));
        System.out.println(
            formatString("hELP", /*INSERT*/));
    }

    private static String formatString(String str,
                    Formatter<String> formatter) {
        return formatter.format(str);
    }
}
```

Which of the following options can replace /*INSERT*/ such that on executing Test class, passed Strings are formatted in Camel case? The output should be:

```
Hello
Help
```

Consider that passed string should be continuous, without any white-spaces in between. Select one option from below.

A.	`s -> s.substring(0, 1).toUpperCase() + s.substring(1).toLowerCase()`
B.	`s -> s.substring(0, 1).toUpperCase() + s.substring(1, 5).toLowerCase()`
C.	`s -> s.toCamelCase()`
D.	Other three options are not correct.

2.1.23 Consider below code:

```java
package com.udayan.lambda;

public class Test {
    public static void main(String[] args) {
        Operation o1 = (x, y) -> x + y;
        System.out.println(o1.operate(5, 10));
    }
}
```

Which of the following functional interface definitions can be used here, so that the output of above code is: 15?
Select ALL that apply.

| A. | ```
interface Operation {
    int operate(int x, int y);
}
``` |
| B. | ```
interface Operation {
    long operate(long x, long y);
}
``` |
| C. | ```
interface Operation<T> {
    T operate(T x, T y);
}
``` |
| D. | ```
interface Operation<T extends Integer> {
    T operate(T x, T y);
}
``` |

2.1.24 What will be the result of compiling and executing Test class?

```java
package com.udayan.lambda;

interface Operation {
    int operate(int x, int y);
}

public class Test {
    public static void main(String[] args) {
        int x = 10;
        int y = 20;
        Operation o1 = (x, y) -> x * y;
        System.out.println(o1.operate(5, 10));
    }
}
```

A. 50

B. 200

C. Compilation error

D. Exception is thrown at runtime

2.1.25 For the code below:

```java
package com.udayan.lambda;

import java.util.Arrays;

public class Test {
    public static void main(String[] args) {
        String [] arr =
            {"**", "***", "*", "*****", "****"};
        Arrays.sort(arr, (s1, s2) ->
            s1.length()-s2.length());
        for(String str : arr) {
            System.out.println(str);
        }
    }
}
```

What do you need to do so that above code gives following output?

```
*
**
***
****
*****
```

A.	Add the import statement for the Comparator interface: **import** java.util.Comparator;
B.	Existing code without any changes displays above output.
C.	Change the lambda expression to (s1, s2) -> s2.length()-s1.length()
D.	Change the lambda expression to (s2, s1) -> s1.length()-s2.length()

2.2 Answers of Practice Test - 2 with Explanation

2.1.1 Answer: C

Reason:
Arrow operator (->) was added in JDK 8 for lambda expressions. NOTE: there should not be any space between - and >.

2.1.2 Answer: A,B,C,D,E

Reason:
print(String) method accepts parameter of String type, so left side of lambda expression should specify one parameter, then arrow operator and right side of lambda expression should specify the body.
(String msg) -> {System.out.println(msg);}; => Correct.
(msg) -> {System.out.println(msg);}; => Correct, type of variable can be removed from left side. Java compiler handles it using type inference.
(msg) -> System.out.println(msg); => Correct, if there is only one statement in the right side then semicolon inside the body, curly brackets and return statement(if available) can be removed.
msg -> System.out.println(msg); => Correct, if there is only one parameter in left part, then round brackets can be removed.
x -> System.out.println(x); => Correct, any valid java identifier can be used in lambda expression.
y - > System.out.println(y); => Compilation error as there should not be any space between - and > of arrow operator.

2.1.3 Answer: A,B,D

Reason:
Operator opr = (int x, int y) -> { return x + y; }; => Correct, operate(int, int) method accepts two int type parameters and returns the addition of passed parameters.
Operator opr = (x, y) -> { return x + y; }; => Correct, type is removed from left part, type inference handles it.
Operator opr = (x, y) -> return x + y; => Compilation error, if there is only one statement in the right side then semicolon inside the body, curly brackets and return statement(if

available) can be removed. But all should be removed. You can't just remove one and leave others.

Operator opr = (x, y) -> x + y; => Correct, semicolon inside the body, curly brackets and return statement, all 3 are removed from right side.

Operator opr = x, y -> x + y; => Compilation error, if there are no parameters or more than one parameter available, then round brackets cannot be removed from left side.

2.1.4 Answer: D

Reason:
Reference variable to which lambda expression is assigned is known as target type. Target type can be a static variable, instance variable, local variable, method parameter or return type. Lambda expression doesn't work without target type and target type must be a functional interface. Functional interface was added in JDK 8 and it contains one non-overriding abstract method.
As Greetings is abstract class, so lambda expression cannot be used in this case.

2.1.5 Answer: D

Reason:
Lambda expression doesn't work without target type and target type must be a functional interface, so in this case as the given lambda expression is not assigned to any target type, hence its purpose is not clear. In fact, given lambda expression causes compilation error without its target type.

2.1.6 Answer: C

Reason:
@FunctionalInterface annotation is used to tag a functional interface.

2.1.7 Answer: B

Reason:
@FunctionalInterface annotation cannot be used here as interface I1 specifies two non-overriding abstract methods. This code causes compilation error.

2.1.8   Answer: B

Reason:
Functional interface must have only one non-overriding abstract method but Functional interface can have constant variables, static methods, default methods and overriding abstract methods [equals(Object) method, toString() method etc. from Object class] I4 is a Functional Interface.

2.1.9   Answer: C

Reason:
Lambda expression is defined correctly but print() method is not invoked on obj reference. So, no output.

2.1.10   Answer: D

Reason:
If curly brackets are removed from lambda expression body, then return keyword should also be removed. There should not be space between - and >.
For one parameter, parentheses or round brackets () can be removed.

2.1.11   Answer: B

Reason:
Functional interface must have one and only one non-overriding abstract method. boolean equals(Object) is declared and defined in Object class, hence it is not non-overriding abstract method.
@FunctionalInterface annotation causes compilation error.

2.1.12   Answer: C

Reason:
Keyword this within anonymous inner class code refers to the instance of anonymous inner class itself, so this.i in anonymous inner class code is 200.
Whereas, keyword this within lambda expression refers to the instance of enclosing class where lambda expression is written, so this.i in lambda expression is 100.

Java Functional Programming - Lambda & Stream Practice Tests

2.1.13 Answer: B

Reason:
Lambda expression is written inside Inner class, so this keyword in lambda expression refers to the instance of Inner class.
Hence, System.out.println(this.var); prints 1000.

2.1.14 Answer: C

Reason:
variable i is a local variable and it is used in the lambda expression. So, it should either be final or effectively final.
The last statement inside main(String []) method, increments value of i, which means it is not effectively final and hence compilation error.

2.1.15 Answer: C

Reason:
No issues with lambda syntax: curly brackets and semicolon are available. Variable i is declared within the body of lambda expression so don't confuse it with local variable of main method. i is declared and initialized to 10, i is incremented by 1 (i becomes 11) and finally value of i is printed.

2.1.16 Answer: B

Reason:
Lambda expression can be assigned to static variable, instance variable, local variable, method parameter or return type. method(I10, String) accepts two arguments, hence method(s -> System.out.println(s.toUpperCase())); would cause compilation error.
When curly brackets are used then semicolon is necessary, hence method(s -> { System.out.println(s.toUpperCase()) }, "good morning!"); would cause compilation error.
method(s -> s.toUpperCase(), "good morning!"); is a legal syntax but, nothing is printed to the console.

2.1.17 Answer: C

Reason:
Dot (.) operator has higher precedence than concatenation operator, hence toUpperCase() is invoked on str2 and not on the result of (str1 + "_" + str2)

2.1.18 Answer: C

Reason:
Operator is a generic interface, hence it can work with any java class. There are absolutely no issues with lambda expressions but we are not capturing or printing the return value of operation method, hence nothing is printed on to the console.
System.out.println(opr1.operation("Hello", "World")); => Prints HelloWorld.
System.out.println(opr2.operation(10, 40)); => Prints 50. Over here int literals 10 and 40 are converted to Integer instances by auto-boxing.

2.1.19 Answer: D

Reason:
Reference variable to which lambda expression is assigned is known as target type. Target type can be a static variable, instance variable, local variable, method parameter or return type. Lambda expression doesn't work without target type and target type must be a functional interface.
In this case, println(Object) method is invoked but Object is a class and not a functional interface, hence no lambda expression can be passed directly to println method.

But you can first assign lambda expression to target type and then pass the target type reference variable to println(Object) method:
Operator<String> operator = (s1, s2) -> s1 + s2;
System.out.println(operator);

Or you can typecast lambda expression to target type. e.g. following works:
System.out.println((Operator<String>)(String s1, String s2) -> s1 + s2);
System.out.println((Operator<String>)(s1, s2) -> s1 + s2);
System.out.println((Operator<String>)(s1, s2) -> { return s1 + s2; });

Java Functional Programming - Lambda & Stream Practice Tests

2.1.20 Answer: A,B,C

Reason:
Comparator has only one non-overriding abstract method, compare. Runnable has only one non-overriding abstract method, run. ActionListener has only one non-overriding abstract method, actionPerformed. Serializable and Cloneable are marker interfaces.

2.1.21 Answer: B,C,D

Reason:
Collections.sort(names, (o1, o2) -> o1.getFirst().compareTo(o2.getFirst())); => It sorts in the ascending order of first name in case-sensitive manner and displays [John Smith, Peter Lee, bonita smith] in the output.
Collections.sort(names, (o1, o2) -> o1.getFirst().toLowerCase().compareTo(o2.getFirst().toLowerCase())); => At the time of comparison, first names in lower case are considered, this doesn't change the case of displayed output. Output is: [bonita smith, John Smith, Peter Lee].
Collections.sort(names, (o1, o2) -> o1.getFirst().toUpperCase().compareTo(o2.getFirst().toUpperCase())); => At the time of comparison, first names in upper case are considered, this doesn't change the case of displayed output. Output is: [bonita smith, John Smith, Peter Lee].
Collections.sort(names, (o1, o2) -> o1.getFirst().compareToIgnoreCase(o2.getFirst())); => compareToIgnoreCase method compares the first names in case-insensitive manner and displays
[bonita smith, John Smith, Peter Lee] in the output.

2.1.22 Answer: A

Reason:
Passed string's first character should be converted to upper case and rest of the characters should be converted to lower case. Combination of substring method with toUpperCase and toLowerCase method does the trick. s.substring(1, 5) will throw StringIndexOutOfBoundsException for "hELP". There is no toCamelCase() method defined in String class.

2.1.23 Answer: A,B,D

Reason:
From the given syntax inside main method, it is clear that interface name is Operation and it has an abstract method operate which accepts 2 parameters of numeric type and returns the numeric result (as result of adding 5 and 10 is 15). So, int and long versions can be easily applied here.
Operation<T> will not work here as inside main method, raw type is used, which means x and y will be of Object type and x + y will cause compilation error as + operator is not defined when both the operands are of Object type.
For Operation<T extends Integer>, even though main method uses raw type, but x and y will be of Integer type and hence x + y will not cause any compilation error.

2.1.24 Answer: C

Reason:
Lambda expression's variables x and y cannot redeclare another local variables defined in the enclosing scope.

2.1.25 Answer: B

Reason:
Even though lambda expression is for the compare method of Comparator interface, but in the code name "Comparator" is not used hence import statement is not needed here.
Expressions
(s1, s2) -> s2.length()-s1.length() and (s2, s1) -> s1.length()-s2.length() displays the output in reversed order.

3 Practice Test-3

3.1 This practice test covers questions on:

- Method reference and its syntax
- Double colon (::) operator
- 4 types of method references:
  - ✓ Method Reference to Constructor
  - ✓ Method Reference to Static Method
  - ✓ Method reference to an Instance Method of a Particular Object
  - ✓ Method Reference to an Instance Method of an Arbitrary Object of a Particular Type
- Possibility of ambiguous call when a method reference syntax refers to both static and instance method of the class

Java Functional Programming - Lambda & Stream Practice Tests

3.1.1 Which of the following operator is used in method references?

A. ->

B. ::

C. : :

D. :->

3.1.2 Consider below code:

```java
package com.udayan.mr;

import java.text.DateFormat;
import java.text.SimpleDateFormat;
import java.util.Date;

@FunctionalInterface
interface Printer {
    void print();
}

class Util {
    public static void printCurrentTime() {
        //Format to display date
        DateFormat dateFormat
            = new SimpleDateFormat("dd-MM-yyyy HH:mm:ss");

        //Create a date object representing
        // current date and time
        Date date = new Date();

        //prints the date object in above format
        System.out.println(dateFormat.format(date));
    }
}

public class Test {
    public static void main(String[] args) {
        Printer creator =
                () -> Util.printCurrentTime();
        creator.print();
    }
}
```

On execution, Test class prints the current date and time on to the console.
Which of the following method reference syntax can replace the Lambda expression [()
-> Util.printCurrentTime();] inside main method such that there is no change in the
output?

A. `Util::printCurrentTime();`

B. `Util::printCurrentTime;`

C. `Util->printCurrentTime();`

D. `Util->printCurrentTime;`

3.1.3 Consider the given code:

```java
package com.udayan.mr;

@FunctionalInterface
interface Operator {
    void operate(int i, int j);
}

class Calculator {
    public static void add(int i, int j) {
        System.out.println(i + j);
    }
}

public class Test {
    public static void main(String[] args) {
        Operator opr = (i, j)
            -> System.out.println(i + j); //Line 14
        opr.operate(15, 25);
    }
}
```

On execution, Test class prints 40 on to the console. Which of the following statements
can replace Line 14 such that there is no change in the output?
Select ALL that apply.

A. Operator opr = Calculator.add(i, j);

B. Operator opr = (i, j) -> Calculator.add(i, j);

C. Operator opr = Calculator::add;

D. Operator opr = Calculator::add(i, j);

3.1.4 What will be the result of compiling and executing Test class?

```
package com.udayan.mr;

interface I02 {
    int f(int i, int j, int k);
}

public class Test {
    private static int cube(int i, int j, int k) {
        return i * j * k;
    }

    public static void main(String[] args) {
        I02 obj = Test::cube;
        System.out.println(obj.f(10, 20, 30));
    }
}
```

A. 6000

B. Compilation error

C. Runtime error

D. None of the other options

3.1.5 What will be the result of compiling and executing Test class?

```java
package com.udayan.mr;

interface Creator<T> {
    T create();
}

class Book {
    public Book() {
        System.out.println(1);
    }

    public String toString() {
        return "2";
    }
}

public class Test {
    public static void main(String[] args) {
        Creator<Book> obj = Book::new;
        obj.create().toString();
    }
}
```

A.	1	B.	2
C.	1 2	D.	Compilation error

3.1.6 What will be the result of compiling and executing Test class?

```java
package com.udayan.mr;

interface Creator<T> {
    T create();
}

abstract class Gift {
    public Gift() {
        super();
    }

    public String toString() {
        return "Gift";
    }
}

class Book extends Gift {
    public Book() {
        super();
    }

    public String toString() {
        return "Book";
    }
}

public class Test {
    public static void main(String[] args) {
        Creator<Gift> obj = Gift::new;
        System.out.println(obj.create());
    }
}
```

A. Compilation error
B. Runtime error
C. Gift
D. Book

3.1.7 What will be the result of compiling and executing Test class?

```java
package com.udayan.mr;

interface Creator<T> {
    T create();
}

enum AnimalType {
    MAMMAL, BIRD, REPTILE;
}

abstract class Animal {
    private AnimalType type;

    public Animal(AnimalType type) {
        this.type = type;
    }

    public AnimalType getType() {
        return type;
    }
}

class Dog extends Animal {
    public Dog(AnimalType type) {
        super(AnimalType.MAMMAL);
    }
}

public class Test {
    public static void main(String[] args) {
        Creator<Dog> obj = Dog::new;
        Dog d = obj.create();
        System.out.println(d.getType());
    }
}
```

A. MAMMAL

B. mammal

C. 0

D. Compilation error

3.1.8 Consider following code:

```java
package com.udayan.mr;

interface I1 {
    void m(int i, int j);
}

class MyClass {
    public void add(int i, int j) {
        System.out.println(i * j);
    }
}

public class Test {
    public static void main(String[] args) {
        MyClass obj = new MyClass();
        I1 i1 = (i, j)
            -> System.out.println(i * j); //Line 16
        i1.m(24, 12);
    }
}
```

On executing Test class, 288 is shown in the console. Which of the following can replace Line 16 such that there is no change in the output?

Select ALL that apply.

A. I1 i1 = (i, j) -> obj.add(i, j);
B. I1 i1 = MyClass::add;
C. I1 i1 = obj::add;
D. I1 i1 = obj.add;

3.1.9 What will be the result of compiling and executing Test class?

```java
package com.udayan.mr;

interface DoubleToByte {
    byte getValue();
}

public class Test {
    public static void main(String[] args) {
        DoubleToByte obj
            = new Double("123")::byteValue;
        System.out.println(obj.getValue());
    }
}
```

A. Compilation error

B. Runtime error

C. 123

D. None of the other options

3.1.10 What will be the result of compiling and executing Test class?

```java
package com.udayan.mr;

interface Creator<T> {
    T create();
}

public class Test {
    public static void main(String[] args) {
        Creator<String> obj
            = process("   abc d")::toUpperCase;
        System.out.println(">" + obj.create() + "<");
    }

    private static String process(String str) {
        return str.trim();
    }
}
```

A. Compilation error

B. >   ABC D<

C. >ABC D<

D. >ABCD<

3.1.11 What will be the result of compiling and executing Test class?

```java
package com.udayan.mr;

interface I10 {
    void print(Object obj);
}

public class Test {
    public static void main(String[] args) {
        I10 obj = System.out::println;
        obj.print("Hello World!");
    }
}
```

A. Compilation error

B. Hello World!

C. Runtime error

D. None of the other options

3.1.12 Consider below expression compiles fine:

```java
I1 obj = (Student s) -> s.getMarks();
```

Which one is the correct method reference syntax for above lambda expression?

A. I1 obj = s::getMarks;

B. I1 obj = Student::getMarks();

C. I1 obj = Student::getMarks;

D. I1 obj = s::getMarks();

3.1.13 Consider below expression compiles fine:

```
SomeInterface obj = (str, index) -> str.substring(index);
```

Which one is the correct method reference syntax for above lambda expression?

A. `SomeInterface obj = s::substring;`
B. `SomeInterface obj = s::substring();`
C. `SomeInterface obj = String::substring;`
D. `SomeInterface obj = String::substring();`

3.1.14 What will be the result of compiling and executing Test class?

```java
package com.udayan.mr;

interface Printable {
    void print(Printer p1, Printer p2);
}

class Printer {
    public static void print(Printer p1, Printer p2) {
        System.out.println(p1.toString()
                            + "$$" + p2.toString());
    }

    public void print(Printer p) {
        System.out.println(p.toString());
    }

    public String toString() {
        return "Hello";
    }
}

public class Test {
    public static void main(String[] args) {
        Printable obj = Printer::print;
        obj.print(new Printer(), new Printer());
    }
}
```

A.	Hello$$Hello	B.	Hello
C.	Hello$$Hello Hello	D.	Compilation error

3.1.15 Consider below code:

```
package com.udayan.mr;

public class Test {
    public static void main(String[] args) {
        I01<Integer> obj = Integer::new;
        System.out.println(obj.create("603"));
    }
}
```

Which of the following functional interface definitions can be used here, so that the output of above code is: 603?

Select ALL that apply.

| A. | ```interface I01 {
    Integer create(String str);
}``` |
|---|---|
| B. | ```interface I01<T> {
    T create(String str);
}``` |
| C. | ```interface I01<T extends Integer> {
    T create(String str);
}``` |
| D. | ```interface I01<T extends Number> {
    T create(String str);
}``` |

3.1.16 What will be the result of compiling and executing TestStudent class?

```java
package com.udayan.mr;
import java.util.ArrayList;
import java.util.Collections;
import java.util.List;

class Student {
    private String name;
    private int age;

    public Student(String name, int age) {
        this.name = name;
        this.age = age;
    }

    public String toString() {
        return "Student (" + name + ", " + age + ")";
    }

    public static int compareByAge(Student s1,
                                   Student s2) {
        return s1.age - s2.age;
    }
}
public class TestStudent {
    public static void main(String[] args) {
        List<Student> students = new ArrayList<>();
        students.add(new Student("john", 25));
        students.add(new Student("lucy", 21));
        students.add(new Student("ivy", 23));

        Collections
            .sort(students, Student::compareByAge);

        System.out.println(students);
    }
}
```

A. Compilation error.

B. [Student (john, 25), Student (ivy, 23), Student (lucy, 21)]

C. [Student (lucy, 21), Student (ivy, 23), Student (john, 25)]

D. An exception is thrown at runtime.

3.1.17 What will be the result of compiling and executing Test class?

```java
package com.udayan.mr;

interface Creator<T, R> {
    R create(T t);
}

class Log {

    Log() {
        System.out.println(1);
    }

    Log(String name) {
        System.out.println(2);
    }

}
public class Test {
    public static void main(String[] args) {
        Creator<String, Log> obj = Log::new;
    }
}
```

A. 1

B. 2

C. It executes fine but no output

D. Compilation error

3.1.18 Which of the following statements are true about Student::new?

A. It is referring to no-argument constructor of Student class.

B. It is referring to parameterized constructor of Student class.

C. It is referring to static method new of Student class.

D. It is referring to instance method new of Student class.

E. Syntax is incomplete to infer anything.

3.1.19 Consider below code:

```
package com.udayan.mr;

interface Operator<T> {
    T operate(T t);
}

public class Test {
    public static void main(String[] args) {
        Operator<String> opr =
            s -> s.toUpperCase(); //Line 7
        System.out.println(opr.operate(
                "lamdba and method references."));
    }
}
```

On execution, above code prints "LAMBDA AND METHOD REFERENCES." on to the console. Which of the following can replace Line 7 such that there is no change in the output?

A. `Operator<String> opr = s.toUpperCase();`

B. `Operator<String> opr = s::toUpperCase();`

C. `Operator<String> opr = s::toUpperCase;`

D. `Operator<String> opr = String::toUpperCase;`

3.1.20 Consider below code:

```java
package com.udayan.mr;

interface Creator<T, R> {
    R create(T t);
}

abstract class Animal {
    abstract void eat();
}

class Dog extends Animal {
    private String name;

    void eat() {
        System.out.println(this.name
                + " eats biscuits.");
    }
}

public class Test {
    public static void main(String[] args) {
        Creator<String, Animal> obj
                = Dog::new; //Line n1
        obj.create("Cooper"); //Line n2
    }
}
```

Line n1 is giving compilation error. Which of the following is NEEDED so that on execution, Test class prints "Cooper eats biscuits." on to the console?

Select ALL that apply.

A.	Add below constructor in the Dog class:
	`Dog(String name) {`
	`    this.name = name;`
	`}`

B.	Add no-argument constructor in the Dog class:
	`Dog() {`
	`    this.name = "Cooper";`
	`}`

C.	Add no-argument constructor in the Animal class: `Animal() {}`
D.	Replace Line n2 with: `obj.create("Cooper").eat();`

3.2 Answers of Practice Test - 3 with Explanation

3.1.1 Answer: B

Reason:
Double colon operator (::) was added in JDK 8 for method references. NOTE: There should not be any space between : and :.

3.1.2 Answer: B

Reason:
This is an example of method reference to static method. Double colon (::) operator is used for method reference syntax. print() method of Printer interface and printCurrentTime() method of Util class don't accept any parameters. () -> Util.printCurrentTime(); is same as Util::printCurrentTime.
NOTE: round brackets are not used in any of the method reference syntax.

3.1.3 Answer: B,C

Reason:
This is an example of method reference to static method. Lambda expressions can invoke helper methods to accomplish their task. "Operator opr = (i, j) -> System.out.println(i + j);" can be changed to "Operator opr = (i, j) -> Calculator.add(i, j);" So, instead of writing the logic in lambda expression, it took the help of static add method of Calculator class. And as a static method is invoked so it is a candidate for method reference syntax. "Operator opr = (i, j) -> Calculator.add(i, j);" can be simplified to "Operator opr = Calculator::add;"

3.1.4 Answer: A

Reason:
This is an example of method reference to static method.
Both method f(int, int, int) and static method cube(int, int, int) have same arguments.
Test::cube is same as (i, j, k) -> Test.cube(i, j, k);
obj.f(10, 20, 30) returns 6000.

3.1.5   Answer: A

Reason:
This is an example of method reference to Constructor. create() method accepts no parameters and there is no-argument constructor in Book class as well, so Book::new is correct syntax for reference to a constructor.
obj.create() invokes the constructor of Book class and hence 1 is printed in the output. toString() method is invoked next, it returns "2" but this value is not passed to println method, hence no output for toString() call.

3.1.6   Answer: A

Reason:
This is an example of method reference to Constructor. Gift is an abstract class and constructor of an abstract class cannot be invoked by using new keyword.
Gift::new causes compilation error.

3.1.7   Answer: D

Reason:
This is an example of method reference to Constructor. create() method accepts no parameters. But no-argument constructor is not available in the Dog class.
As parameters of create() method and Dog(AnimalType) constructor do not match, hence Dog::new causes compilation error.

3.1.8   Answer: A,C

Reason:
This is the case of "Reference to an Instance Method of a Particular Object".
Body of lambda expression can invoke instance method as well and this is what "I1 i1 = (i, j) -> obj.add(i, j);" is doing. Lambda parameters and add method parameters are same so this expression can be simplified further to: "I1 i1 = obj::add;". Other options are incorrect.

Java Functional Programming - Lambda & Stream Practice Tests

3.1.9   Answer: C

Reason:
This is the case of "Reference to an Instance Method of a Particular Object".
getValue() method of DoubleToByte interface and byteValue() method of Double class don't accept any arguments.
So, left side of method reference syntax, can be any of the following:
A reference variable of Double type, a method which returns Double or a Double constructor call.
So, new Double("123")::byteValue is a perfectly valid syntax.
obj.getValue() returns the corresponding byte value 123.

3.1.10   Answer: C

Reason:
This is the case of "Reference to an Instance Method of a Particular Object".
create() method doesn't specify and parameter and toUpperCase() method of String class also doesn't accept any argument.
So, left side of method reference syntax, can be any of the following:
A String reference variable, A String literal, An expression resulting to String object, a method call which returns String or String constructor call.
In this case, process method returns String object, so it can be used in method reference syntax.
Note: trim() method trims the leading and trailing white spaces and not the spaces in between.

3.1.11   Answer: B

Reason:
This is the case of "Reference to an Instance Method of a Particular Object".
Both print(Object) method and println(Object) method accepts same argument.
System.out::println means println method is called on System.out reference variable.
obj.print("Hello World!"); invokes System.out.println("Hello World!"); and this prints Hello World! to the console.

3.1.12 Answer: C

Reason:
This is an example of "Reference to an Instance Method of an Arbitrary Object of a Particular Type".
Parameter of lambda expression is used to invoke the getMarks() method and getMarks() method doesn't accept any parameter.
So, correct method reference syntax is: Student::getMarks;
Note round brackets are not used in any of the method reference syntax.

3.1.13 Answer: C

Reason:
This is an example of "Reference to an Instance Method of an Arbitrary Object of a Particular Type".
First parameter of lambda expression is used to invoke the substring() method and substring() method accepts one parameter, which is same as the 2nd parameter of lambda expression.
So, correct method reference syntax is: String::substring;
Note round brackets are not used in any of the method reference syntax.

3.1.14 Answer: D

Reason:
Printer::print is an ambiguous call and it refers to both the static and instance method of class A:
Printable obj = (p1, p2) -> A.print(p1, p2); and Printable obj = (p1, p2) -> p1.print(p2);

So Printer::print causes compilation error.

3.1.15 Answer: B,C,D

Reason:
Following points are deduced by the given code:
1. By looking at the statement, I01<Integer> obj = Integer::new; you can say that interface name should be I01 and it should be a generic interface.
2. Expression obj.create("603") tells that single abstract method (SAM) of interface should be named as "create" and it should specify one String parameter.
3. As obj.create("603") is used as an argument of println method, this means return type of create method can't be void. It should return some object.
4. Integer(String){...} constructor of Integer class converts String to an Integer, so constructor reference Integer::new refers to this constructor. This means obj.create("603") should return an Integer object.

Based on above deduction correct options can be easily selected.

3.1.16 Answer: C

Reason:
Collections.sort(students, Student::compareByAge); The second argument of Collections.sort method expects a Comparator(FunctionalInterface) instance. As first argument of sort method is list of Student, hence compare method of Comparator should accept 2 parameters of Student type and returns an int value. This is what static compareByAge method of Student class does and hence its reference can be used as 2nd argument to Collections.sort method.

All needed import statements are available, as name "Comparator" is not referred in the code hence statement import java.util.Comparator; is not needed.

3.1.17 Answer: C

Reason:
Log::new; is same as s -> new Log(s);
As create method accepts first type parameter T, which is String and returns 2nd type parameter R, which is Log. So, lambda expression s -> new Log(s); calls the parameterized constructor of Log class and returns the Log instance.

But to create an instance of Log class, you need to invoke the create method:
obj.create("some string");

3.1.18 Answer: E

Reason:
Method name cannot be new as new is a java keyword and not a valid identifier.
Student::new can refer to no-argument or parameterized constructor of Student class but unless target type is available you cannot be sure about it.

3.1.19 Answer: D

Reason:
This is an example of "Reference to an Instance Method of an Arbitrary Object of a Particular Type".
Parameter of lambda expression is used to invoke the toUpperCase() method and toUpperCase() method accepts no parameter, which means one parameter less than the operate method.
So, correct method reference syntax is: String::toUpperCase;
Note round brackets are not used in any of the method reference syntax.

3.1.20 Answer: A,D

Reason:
Question is asking about NEEDED statements. Line n1 indicates that Dog's class constructor must accept String argument (check the create method signature of Creator).
Adding parameterized constructor in Dog class will rectify the compilation error and on execution it will assign Cooper to name variable. But to print "Cooper eats biscuits.", eat() method should be invoked. So, invoke eat() method in Line n2. After making these 2 changes, even if you provide no-argument constructors in Dog and Animal class, it will not affect the output so not needed as well.

4 Practice Test-4

4.1 This practice test covers questions on:

- Supplier interface
- Consumer interface and its default method: andThen
- Predicate interface and its default methods: and, or, negate
- Function interface and its default methods: compose, andThen
- Comparator interface, its static method: comparing and default methods: thenComparing, reversed

4.1.1 Built-in functional interfaces are part of which java package?

A. java.lang
B. java.util
C. java.util.function
D. java.function

4.1.2 Which of the following pairs correctly represents the Functional interface and its single abstract method?

A.	Consumer : apply Function : accept Supplier : test Predicate : get	B.	Consumer : apply Function : accept Supplier : get Predicate : test
C.	Consumer : accept Function : apply Supplier : get Predicate : test	D.	Consumer : accept Function : apply Supplier : test Predicate : get

4.1.3 What will be the result of compiling and executing Test class?

```java
package com.udayan.fi;

import java.util.function.Supplier;

public class Test {
    public static void main(String[] args) {
        Supplier<StringBuilder> supplier = () ->
            new StringBuilder(" olleH").reverse()
                        .append("!dlroW").reverse();
        System.out.println(supplier.get());
    }
}
```

A. >World! olleH<

B. >Hello World!<

C. > olleHWorld!<

D. > olleH!dlroW<

E. >World!Hello <

4.1.4 Consider below code:

```java
package com.udayan.fi;

import java.util.Date;
import java.util.function.*;

public class Test {
    public static void main(String[] args) {
        //Constructor reference for Date() constructor
        /*INSERT*/ obj = Date::new;

        //Creates an instance of Date class.
        Date date = obj.get();
        System.out.println(date);
    }
}
```

Which of the following options can replace /*INSERT*/ such that on executing Test class, current date and time is displayed in the output?

A. Supplier
B. Supplier<Object>
C. Supplier<Date>
D. Function
E. Function<Date>
F. Function<Object>

4.1.5 You have to create below functional interface:

```
interface Generator<T, U> {
    U generate(T t);
}
```

Which of the following built-in interface you can use instead of above interface.

A. Supplier
B. Function
C. Predicate
D. Consumer

4.1.6 What will be the result of compiling and executing Test class?

```java
package com.udayan.fi;

import java.util.function.Function;

public class Test {
    public static void main(String[] args) {
        Function<char [], String> obj
                    = String::new; //Line 5
        String s = obj.apply(
            new char[] {'j', 'a', 'v', 'a'}); //Line 6
        System.out.println(s);
    }
}
```

A. java

B. Compilation error at Line 5

C. Compilation error at Line 6

D. Exception is thrown at runtime

4.1.7 Consider below code:

```java
package com.udayan.fi;

import java.util.function.Function;

public class Test {
    public static void main(String[] args) {
        Function<Integer, Integer> f = x -> x + 10;
        Function<Integer, Integer> g = y -> y * y;

        Function<Integer, Integer> fog
                        = g.compose(f); //Line 8
        System.out.println(fog.apply(10));
    }
}
```

On execution, Test class prints 400 on to the console. Which of the statements can replace Line 8 such that there is no change in the output?

A. Function<Integer, Integer> fog = f.compose(g);

B. Function<Integer, Integer> fog = f.andThen(g);

C. Function<Integer, Integer> fog = g.andThen(f);

4.1.8 What will be the result of compiling and executing Test class?

```
package com.udayan.fi;

import java.util.function.Function;

public class Test {
    public static void main(String[] args) {
        Function<String, Integer> f1 = Integer::new;
        Function<String, String> f2 = s ->
            new StringBuilder(s).reverse().toString();
        System.out.println(f1.compose(f2).apply("12345"));
    }
}
```

A. 12345

B. 54321

C. Compilation error

D. NumberFormatException is thrown at runtime

4.1.9 What will be the result of compiling and executing Test class?

```java
package com.udayan.fi;

import java.util.function.Predicate;

public class Test {
    public static void main(String[] args) {
        printNumbers(i -> i % 2 != 0);
    }

    private static void printNumbers(
                Predicate<Integer> predicate) {
        for(int i = 1; i <= 10; i++) {
            if(predicate.test(i)) {
                System.out.print(i);
            }
        }
    }
}
```

A. 12345678910
B. 1234567891011
C. 246810
D. 13579
E. 1357911

4.1.10 What will be the result of compiling and executing Test class?

```java
package com.udayan.fi;

import java.util.function.Predicate;

public class Test {
    public static void main(String[] args) {
        String [] arr = {"*", "**", "***", "****",
                        "*****", "******"};
        Predicate<String> pr1 = s -> s.length() > 3;
        print(arr, pr1.negate());
    }

    private static void print(String [] arr,
                              Predicate<String> predicate) {
        for(String str : arr) {
            if(predicate.test(str)) {
                System.out.println(str);
            }
        }
    }
}
```

A.	**** ***** ******	B.	* ** ***
C.	* **	D.	* ** *** **** ***** ******

4.1.11 What will be the result of compiling and executing Test class?

```java
package com.udayan.fi;

import java.util.Arrays;
import java.util.Comparator;

public class Test {
    public static void main(String[] args) {
        String [] arr = {"A5", "B4", "C3", "D2", "E1"};
        Arrays.sort(arr,
            Comparator.comparing(s -> s.substring(1)));
        for(String str : arr) {
            System.out.print(str + " ");
        }
    }
}
```

A. E1 D2 C3 B4 A5

B. A5 B4 C3 D2 E1

C. A1 B2 C3 D4 E5

D. E5 D4 C3 B2 A1

4.1.12 What will be the result of compiling and executing Test class?

```java
package com.udayan.fi;

import java.util.Arrays;
import java.util.Collections;
import java.util.Comparator;
import java.util.List;

public class Test {
    public static void main(String[] args) {
        List<String> emails = Arrays.asList(
            "udayan@outlook.com", "sachin@outlook.com",
            "sachin@gmail.com", "udayan@gmail.com");
        Collections.sort(emails, Comparator.comparing(
            str -> str.substring(str.indexOf("@") + 1)));
        for(String email : emails) {
            System.out.println(email);
        }
    }
}
```

A.	sachin@gmail.com udayan@gmail.com sachin@outlook.com udayan@outlook.com	B.	sachin@gmail.com udayan@gmail.com udayan@outlook.com sachin@outlook.com
C.	sachin@outlook.com udayan@outlook.com sachin@gmail.com udayan@gmail.com	D.	sachin@outlook.com udayan@outlook.com udayan@gmail.com sachin@gmail.com

4.1.13 What will be the result of compiling and executing Test class?

```java
package com.udayan.fi;

import java.util.function.Consumer;

public class Test {
    public static void main(String[] args) {
        Consumer<String> c1 = str -> {
            System.out.println(new StringBuilder(str)
                    .reverse().toString().substring(2));
        };
        c1.accept("!yppahnu");
    }
}
```

A. ppahnu

B. unhapp

C. !yppah

D. happy!

4.1.14 What will be the result of compiling and executing Test class?

```java
package com.udayan.fi;

import java.util.function.Consumer;

public class Test {
    public static void main(String[] args) {
        Consumer<Integer> consumer = System.out::print;
        Integer i = 5;
        consumer.andThen(consumer).accept(i++); //Line 7
    }
}
```

A. 55

B. 56

C. 66

D. Compilation error

4.1.15 What will be the result of compiling and executing Test class?

```java
package com.udayan.fi;

import java.util.function.Consumer;

class Counter {
    static int count = 1;
}

public class Test {
    public static void main(String[] args) {
        Consumer<Integer> add = i -> Counter.count += i;
        Consumer<Integer> print = System.out::println;
        add.andThen(print).accept(10); //Line 10
    }
}
```

A. 11

B. 10

C. 1

D. Compilation error

4.1.16 What will be the result of compiling and executing Test class?

```java
package com.udayan.fi;

import java.util.function.Predicate;

public class Test {
    public static void main(String[] args) {
        String [] arr = {"A", "ab", "bab", "Aa", "bb",
                        "baba", "aba", "Abab"};

        Predicate<String> p1 = s -> s.startsWith("A");
        Predicate<String> p2 = s -> s.startsWith("a");
        Predicate<String> p3 = s -> s.length() >= 3;

        processStringArray(arr, p1.or(p2).and(p3));
    }

    private static void processStringArray(String [] arr,
                            Predicate<String> predicate) {
        for(String str : arr) {
            if(predicate.test(str)) {
                System.out.println(str);
            }
        }
    }
}
```

A.	Abab	B.	aba Abab
C.	bab baba aba Abab	D.	A ab Aa aba Abab

4.1.17 Consider below code:

```java
package com.udayan.fi;

import java.util.function.Predicate;

public class Test {
    public static void main(String[] args) {
        String [] arr = {"A", "ab", "bab", "Aa",
                        "bb", "baba", "aba", "Abab"};

        processStringArray(arr, /*INSERT*/);
    }

    private static void processStringArray(String [] arr,
                        Predicate<String> predicate) {
        for(String str : arr) {
            if(predicate.test(str)) {
                System.out.println(str);
            }
        }
    }
}
```

Which of the following options can replace /*INSERT*/ such that on executing Test class all the array elements are displayed in the output?
Select ALL that apply.

A. p -> true
B. p -> !false
C. p -> p.length() >= 1
D. p -> p.length() < 10

4.1.18 A bank's swift code is generally of 11 characters and used in international money transfers.

An example: ICICINBBRT4

ICIC: First 4 letters for bank code

IN: Next 2 letters for Country code

Java Functional Programming - Lambda & Stream Practice Tests

BB: Next 2 letters for Location code
RT4: Next 3 letters for Branch code

Consider below code:

```java
package com.udayan.fi;

import java.util.Arrays;
import java.util.Collections;
import java.util.Comparator;
import java.util.List;

public class SortSwiftCode {
    public static void main(String[] args) {
        List<String> swiftCodes
            = Arrays.asList("ICICINDD016", "ICICINBBRT4",
                            "BOTKINDD075", "BARBINBB011",
                            "SBBJINDD062", "ABNATHBK865",
                            "BKCHTHBK012");

        Comparator<String> countryLocationBank = Comparator
            .comparing(SortSwiftCode::extractCountry)
            .thenComparing(SortSwiftCode::extractLocation)
            .thenComparing(SortSwiftCode::extractBank);

        Collections.sort(swiftCodes, countryLocationBank);
        printCodes(swiftCodes);
    }

    private static String extractCountry(String swiftCode)
    {
        return swiftCode.substring(4, 6);
    }

    private static String extractLocation(String swiftCode)
    {
        return swiftCode.substring(6, 8);
    }

    private static String extractBank(String swiftCode)
    {
        return swiftCode.substring(0, 4);
    }

    private static void printCodes(List<String> list)
```

```
    {
        for (String str : list) {
            System.out.println(str);
        }
    }
}
```

What will be the result of compiling and executing Test class?

A.	ABNATHBK865 BKCHTHBK012 BARBINBB011 ICICINBBRT4 BOTKINDD075 ICICINDD016 SBBJINDD062	B.	BARBINBB011 ICICINBBRT4 BOTKINDD075 ICICINDD016 SBBJINDD062 ABNATHBK865 BKCHTHBK012
C.	BARBINBB011 BOTKINDD075 ICICINBBRT4 ICICINDD016 SBBJINDD062 ABNATHBK865 BKCHTHBK012	D.	None of the other options

4.1.19 What will be the result of compiling and executing Test class?

```java
package com.udayan.fi;

import java.util.Arrays;
import java.util.Collections;
import java.util.Comparator;
import java.util.List;

public class Test {
    public static void main(String[] args) {
        List<String> list = Arrays.asList(
                "#####", "#", "##", "####", "###");
        Comparator<String> comp
                = Comparator.comparing(s -> s);
        Collections.sort(list, comp.reversed());
        printCodes(list);

    }

    private static void printCodes(List<String> list) {
        for (String str : list) {
            System.out.println(str);
        }
    }
}
```

A.	`#####`
	`#`
	`##`
	`####`
	`###`
		B.	`###`
			`####`
			`##`
			`#`
			`#####`

C.	`#####`
	`####`
	`###`
	`##`
	`#`
		D.	`#`
			`##`
			`###`
			`####`
			`#####`

4.1.20 Which of the import statements correctly imports the functional interface Comparator?

A. `import java.util.function.Comparator;`
B. `import java.util.Comparator;`
C. `import java.function.Comparator;`
D. `import java.lang.Comparator;`

4.2 Answers of Practice Test - 4 with Explanation

4.1.1 Answer: C

Reason:
All the built-in functional interfaces are defined inside java.util.function package.

4.1.2 Answer: C

Reason:
It is always handy to remember the names and methods of four important built-in functional interfaces:
Supplier<T> : T get();
Function<T, R> : R apply(T t);
Consumer<T> : void accept(T t);
Predicate<T> : boolean test(T t);
Rest of the built-in functional interfaces are either similar to or dependent upon these four interfaces.

4.1.3 Answer: A

Reason:
Syntax is correct and without any errors. Methods are chained from left to right.
new StringBuilder(" olleH") => " olleH"
" olleH".reverse() => "Hello "
"Hello ".append("!dlroW") => "Hello !dlroW"
"Hello !dlroW".reverse() => "World! olleH"

4.1.4 Answer: C

Reason:
Date date = obj.get(); means get() method of the interface is invoked. get() method is declared in Supplier interface. All options of Function interface are incorrect.
Supplier interface's declaration is: public interface Supplier<T> { T get(); }. Note: No parameters are specified in get() method, this means no-argument constructor of Date class is invoked by Date::new. So, Supplier<Date> can replace /*INSERT*/. If you use raw type, Supplier or parameterized type Supplier<Object>, then obj.get() method would return Object type. So Date date = obj.get(); will have to be converted to Date date = (Date)obj.get(); but you are allowed to replace /*INSERT*/ only, hence Supplier and Supplier<Object> are incorrect options.

4.1.5 Answer: B

Reason:
It is always handy to remember the names and methods of four important built-in functional interfaces:
Supplier<T> : T get();
Function<T, R> : R apply(T t);
Consumer<T> : void accept(T t);
Predicate<T> : boolean test(T t);
Rest of the built-in functional interfaces are either similar to or dependent upon these four interfaces.

Clearly, interface Function can be used instead or defining Generator interface.

4.1.6 Answer: A

Reason:
String::new is the constructor reference for String(char []) constructor and obj.apply(new char[] {'j', 'a', 'v', 'a'}); would call the constructor at runtime, converting char [] to String. Variable s refers "java".
If you have issues in understanding method reference syntax, then try to write the corresponding lambda expression first. For example, at Line 5, I have to write a lambda expression which accepts char [] and returns String object. It can be written as:

Function<char [], String> obj2 = arr -> new String(arr); It is bit easier to understand this syntax.

4.1.7 Answer: B

Reason:
compose & andThen are default methods defined in Function interface. Starting with JDK 8, interfaces can define default and static methods.
g.compose(f); means first apply f and then g. Same result is achieved by f.andThen(g); => first apply f and then g.
f.apply(10) = 10 + 10 = 20 and g.apply(20) = 20 * 20 = 400.

4.1.8 Answer: B

Reason:
f1.compose(f2) means first apply f2 and then f1.
f2.apply("12345") returns "54321" and then f1.apply("54321") returns 54321

4.1.9 Answer: D

Reason:
In the boolean expression (predicate.test(i)): i is of primitive int type but auto-boxing feature converts it to Integer wrapper type.
test(Integer) method of Predicate returns true if passed number is an odd number, so given loop prints only odd numbers. for loops works for the numbers from 1 to 10.

4.1.10 Answer: B

Reason:
Lambda expression for Predicate is: s -> s.length() > 3. This means return true if passed string's length is > 3.
pr1.negate() means return true if passed string's length is <= 3. So first three array elements are printed.

4.1.11 Answer: A

Reason:
Sorting is working on 2nd letter of the array elements, which means 5, 4, 3, 2, 1. Sorting is in ascending order (1, 2, 3, 4, 5) hence the output is: E1 D2 C3 B4 A5

4.1.12 Answer: B

Reason:
Comparator is comparing on the basis of email domain: gmail.com and outlook.com.
Insertion order is:
udayan@outlook.com
sachin@outlook.com
sachin@gmail.com
udayan@gmail.com

gmail records should appear before outlook records. So sorting order is:
sachin@gmail.com
udayan@gmail.com
udayan@outlook.com
sachin@outlook.com

NOTE: It is not specified, what to do in case email domain is matching. So, for matching email domain, records are left at insertion order.

4.1.13 Answer: D

Reason:
Consumer<T> interface has void accept(T) method, which means in this case, Consumer<String> interface has void accept(String) method. Given lambda expression accepts String argument and does some operation. First String is converted to StringBuilder object to use the reverse method. new StringBuilder("!yppahnu").reverse().toString() returns "unhappy!" and "unhappy!".substring(2) returns "happy!", which is printed by System.out.println method.

4.1.14 Answer: A

Reason:
andThen is the default method defined in Consumer interface, so it is invoked on consumer reference variable. Value passed in the argument of accept method is passed to both the consumer objects. So, for understanding purpose Line 7 can be split into: consumer.accept(5); consumer.accept(5); It prints 55 on to the console.
Check the code of andThen Consumer interface to understand it better.

4.1.15 Answer: B

Reason:
andThen is the default method defined in Consumer interface, so it is invoked on consumer reference variable. Value passed in the argument of accept method is passed to both the consumer objects. So, for understanding purpose Line 10 can be split into: add.accept(10); print.accept(10); add.accept(10) is executed first and it increments the count variable by 10, so count becomes 11. Then print.accept(10); method prints 10 on to the console.
Check the code of andThen Consumer interface to understand it better.

4.1.16 Answer: B

Reason:
"or" and "and" method of Predicate interface works just like short-circuit || and && operators. p1.or(p2) will return {"A", "ab", "Aa", "aba", "Abab"} and after that and method will retrieve strings of length greater than or equal to 3, this means you would get {"aba", "Abab"} as the final result.

4.1.17 Answer: A,B,C,D

Reason:
p -> true means test method returns true for the passed String.
p -> !false means test method returns true for the passed String.
p -> p.length() >= 1 means test method returns true if passed String's length is greater than or equal to 1 and this is true for all the array elements.
p -> p.length() < 10 means test method returns true if passed String's length is less than 10 and this is true for all the array elements.

4.1.18   Answer: B

Reason:
Default thenComparing method helps to chain the Comparators. First the list is sorted on the basis of country code, if matching country code is found then sorted on the basis of location code and if location code matches then list is sorted on bank code.

4.1.19   Answer: C

Reason:
Comparator.comparing(s -> s); compares the passed Strings only. As all the characters in the String are '#', this means strings are sorted on the basis of their lengths. Comparator referred by comp sorts on the basis of strings' lengths. Default reversed() method just reverses the ordering of the Comparator referred by comp, which means sorts the strings in descending order of their lengths.

4.1.20   Answer: B

Reason:
java.util.Comparator interface is available with Java since JDK 1.2. So, even though it is a functional interface but Java guys didn't move it to java.util.function package. Had Comparator interface moved to java.util.function package, then millions of lines of existing Java codes would have broken. That's why package of all the existing functional interface was not changed.

5 Practice Test-5

5.1 This practice test covers questions on:
- Generic Stream interface and its primitive counterparts
- Creating sequential streams
- Important methods of Stream interface
- Generic Optional class and its primitive counterparts
- Convert arrays and collections to streams
- Sort a collection using Stream API

Java Functional Programming - Lambda & Stream Practice Tests

5.1.1 Given code of Test.java file:

```java
package com.udayan.stream;

import java.util.stream.Stream;

public class Test {
    public static void main(String[] args) {
        Stream<StringBuilder> stream = Stream.of();
        stream.map(s -> s.reverse())
            .forEach(System.out::println);
    }
}
```

What will be the result of compiling and executing Test class?

A. Compilation error

B. NullPointerException is thrown at runtime

C. ClassCastException is thrown at runtime

D. Program executes successfully but nothing is printed on to the console

5.1.2 Given code of Test.java file:

```java
package com.udayan.stream;

import java.util.stream.Stream;

public class Test {
    public static void main(String[] args) {
        Stream.of().map(s -> s.reverse())
            .forEach(System.out::println);
    }
}
```

What will be the result of compiling and executing Test class?

A. Compilation error

B. NullPointerException is thrown at runtime

C. ClassCastException is thrown at runtime

D. Program executes successfully but nothing is printed on to the console

5.1.3 Given code of Test.java file:

```java
package com.udayan.stream;

import java.util.stream.Stream;

public class Test {
    public static void main(String[] args) {
        Stream.of(true, false, true)
                .map(b -> b.toString().toUpperCase())
                .peek(System.out::println);
    }
}
```

What will be the result of compiling and executing Test class?

A.	Compilation error
B.	TRUE FALSE TRUE
C.	true false true
D.	Program executes successfully but nothing is printed on to the console

5.1.4 Given code of Test.java file:

```java
package com.udayan.stream;

import java.util.stream.IntStream;

public class Test {
    public static void main(String[] args) {
        IntStream stream = "OCP".chars();
        stream.forEach(c -> System.out.print((char)c));
        System.out.println(stream.count()); //Line 9
    }
}
```

What will be the result of compiling and executing Test class?

A. OCP3
B. Runtime exception
C. Compilation error
D. None of the other options

5.1.5 Given code of Test.java file:

```java
package com.udayan.stream;

import java.util.stream.Stream;

public class Test {
    public static void main(String[] args) {
        Stream.of(true, false, true)
            .map(b -> b.toString().toUpperCase())
            .peek(System.out::println).count();
    }
}
```

What will be the result of compiling and executing Test class?

A.	TRUE FALSE TRUE 3	B.	TRUE FALSE TRUE
C.	true false true 3	D.	true false true

5.1.6 Given code of Test.java file:

```java
package com.udayan.stream;

import java.util.ArrayList;
import java.util.List;

public class Test {
    public static void main(String[] args) {
        List<String> list = new ArrayList<>();
        System.out.println(list.stream()
                .anyMatch(s -> s.length() > 0));
        System.out.println(list.stream()
                .allMatch(s -> s.length() > 0));
        System.out.println(list.stream()
                .noneMatch(s -> s.length() > 0));
    }
}
```

What will be the result of compiling and executing Test class?

A.	false false false	B.	true true true
C.	false true true	D.	true false false

5.1.7 Given code of Test.java file:

```java
package com.udayan.stream;

import java.util.stream.Stream;

public class Test {
    public static void main(String[] args) {
        Stream<Double> stream = Stream.generate(
                () -> new Double("1.0")).limit(10);
        System.out.println(stream.filter(d -> d > 2)
                                .allMatch(d -> d == 2));
    }
}
```

What will be the result of compiling and executing Test class?

A. false

B. true

5.1.8 Given code of Test.java file:

```java
package com.udayan.stream;

import java.util.stream.Stream;

public class Test {
    public static void main(String[] args) {
        Stream<Integer> stream
                = Stream.iterate(1, i -> i + 1);
        System.out.println(stream.anyMatch(i -> i > 1));
    }
}
```

What will be the result of compiling and executing Test class?

A. true

B. false

C. Nothing is printed on to the console as code runs infinitely

D. true is printed on to the console and code runs infinitely

Java Functional Programming - Lambda & Stream Practice Tests

5.1.9   Given code of Test.java file:

```java
package com.udayan.stream;

import java.util.ArrayList;
import java.util.List;

public class Test {
    public static void main(String[] args) {
        int ref = 10;
        List<Integer> list = new ArrayList<>();
        list.stream().anyMatch(i -> {
            System.out.println("HELLO");
            return i > ref;
        });
    }
}
```

What will be the result of compiling and executing Test class?

A. HELLO

B. Compilation error

C. Program executes successfully but nothing is printed on to the console.

5.1.10   Given code of Test.java file:

```java
package com.udayan.stream;

import java.util.ArrayList;
import java.util.List;

public class Test {
    public static void main(String[] args) {
        int ref = 10;
        List<Integer> list = new ArrayList<>();
        list.stream().anyMatch(i -> {
            System.out.println("HELLO");
            return i > ++ref;
        });
    }
}
```

What will be the result of compiling and executing Test class?

A. HELLO

B. Compilation error

C. Program executes successfully but nothing is printed on to the console.

5.1.11 Given code of Test.java file:

```java
package com.udayan.stream;

import java.util.Optional;
import java.util.stream.Stream;

public class Test {
    public static void main(String[] args) {
        Optional<String> optional = Stream.of("red",
            "green", "blue", "yellow")
            .sorted().findFirst();
        System.out.println(optional.get());
    }
}
```

What will be the result of compiling and executing Test class?

A. red

B. blue

C. green

D. yellow

5.1.12 Given code of Test.java file:

```java
package com.udayan.stream;

import java.util.stream.Stream;

public class Test {
    public static void main(String[] args) {
        Stream<Double> stream = Stream.generate(
                                () -> new Double("1.0"));
        System.out.println(stream.sorted().findFirst());
    }
}
```

What will be the result of compiling and executing Test class?

A. Optional[1.0] is printed and program terminates successfully.

B. Optional[1.0] is printed and program runs infinitely.

C. Nothing is printed and program runs infinitely.

D. Compilation error.

5.1.13 Given code of Test.java file:

```java
package com.udayan.stream;

import java.util.HashMap;
import java.util.Map;

public class Test {
    public static void main(String[] args) {
        Map<Integer, String> map = new HashMap<>();
        map.put(1, "ONE");
        map.put(2, "TWO");
        map.put(3, "THREE");

        System.out.println(map.stream().count());
    }
}
```

What will be the result of compiling and executing Test class?

A. 3

B. 6

C. Runtime Exception

D. Compilation error

5.1.14 Given code of Test.java file:

```java
package com.udayan.stream;

import java.util.ArrayList;
import java.util.Arrays;
import java.util.List;

public class Test {
    public static void main(String[] args) {
        List<String> list = new ArrayList<>
                (Arrays.asList("Z", "Y", "X"));
        list.stream().sorted().findFirst().get();
        System.out.println(list.get(2));
    }
}
```

What will be the result of compiling and executing Test class?

A. X

B. Z

C. Y

D. Runtime Exception

5.1.15 Given code of Test.java file:

```java
package com.udayan.stream;
import java.util.Optional;
import java.util.stream.Stream;

public class Test {
    public static void main(String[] args) {
        Optional<Integer> optional
                    = Stream.of(10).findFirst();
        System.out.println(optional);
    }
}
```

What will be the result of compiling and executing Test class?

A. 10

B. Optional[10]

C. Text containing @ symbol

5.1.16 Given code of Test.java file:

```java
package com.udayan.stream;
import java.util.Optional;

public class Test {
    public static void main(String[] args) {
        Optional<Integer> optional = Optional.of(null);
        System.out.println(optional);
    }
}
```

What will be the result of compiling and executing Test class?

A. Optional.empty

B. Optional[null]

C. Optional[0]

D. NullPointerException is thrown at runtime

5.1.17 Given code of Test.java file:

```java
package com.udayan.stream;

import java.util.Optional;

public class Test {
    public static void main(String[] args) {
        Optional<Integer> optional
                    = Optional.ofNullable(null);
        System.out.println(optional);
    }
}
```

What will be the result of compiling and executing Test class?

A. Optional.empty
B. Optional[null]
C. Optional[0]
D. NullPointerException is thrown at runtime

5.1.18 Given code of Test.java file:

```java
package com.udayan.stream;

import java.util.Optional;
import java.util.stream.Stream;

public class Test {
    public static void main(String[] args) {
        Stream<Number> stream = Stream.of();
        Optional<Number> optional = stream.findFirst();
        System.out.println(optional.orElse(-1));
    }
}
```

What will be the result of compiling and executing Test class?

A. null
B. 0
C. -1
D. Optional.empty

5.1.19 Given code of Test.java file:

```java
package com.udayan.stream;

import java.util.Optional;

public class Test {
    public static void main(String[] args) {
        Optional<Integer> optional
                = Optional.of(null); //Line 8
        System.out.println(optional.orElse(-1)); //Line 9
    }
}
```

What will be the result of compiling and executing Test class?

A. null
B. -1
C. Line 8 throws NullPointerException
D. Line 9 throws NullPointerException

5.1.20 Given code of Test.java file:

```java
package com.udayan.stream;

import java.util.Optional;
import java.util.function.Predicate;
import java.util.stream.Stream;

public class Test {
    public static void main(String[] args) {
        Stream<String> stream = Stream.of("and", "Or",
                    "not", "Equals", "unary", "binary");
        Optional<String> optional = stream.filter(
                ((Predicate<String>)Test::isFirstCharVowel)
                .negate()).findFirst();
        System.out.println(optional.get());
    }

    private static boolean isFirstCharVowel(String str) {
        str = str.substring(0, 1).toUpperCase();
        switch(str) {
            case "A":
            case "E":
            case "I":
            case "O":
            case "U":
                return true;
        }
        return false;
    }
}
```

What will be the result of compiling and executing Test class?

A. and

B. not

C. binary

D. Or

5.1.21 Given code of Test.java file:

```java
package com.udayan.stream;

import java.util.stream.Stream;

public class Test {
    public static void main(String[] args) {
        System.out.println(Stream.of(10, 0, -10)
                        .sorted().findAny().orElse(-1));
    }
}
```

Which of the following statements are true about the execution of Test class? Select ALL that apply.

A. It can print any number from the stream.

B. It will always print 10 on to the console.

C. It will always print -10 on to the console.

D. It will always print 0 on to the console.

E. It will never print -1 on to the console.

5.1.22 Given code of Test.java file:

```java
package com.udayan.stream;

import java.time.LocalDate;
import java.util.Optional;
import java.util.stream.Stream;

public class Test {
    public static void main(String[] args) {
        Stream<LocalDate> stream = Stream.of(
            LocalDate.of(2018, 1, 1),
            LocalDate.of(2018, 1, 1));
        Optional<LocalDate> optional
                = stream.distinct().findAny();

        System.out.println(optional.isPresent() + " : "
                                + optional.get());
    }
}
```

What will be the result of compiling and executing Test class?

A. true : 2018-1-1

B. true : 2018-01-01

C. false : 2018-1-1

D. false : 2018-01-01

5.1.23 Given code of Test.java file:

```java
package com.udayan.stream;

import java.util.OptionalLong;

public class Test {
    public static void main(String[] args) {
        OptionalLong optional = OptionalLong.empty();
        System.out.println(optional.isPresent()
                    + " : " + optional.getAsLong());
    }
}
```

What will be the result of compiling and executing Test class?

A. true : 0
B. false : 0
C. false : null
D. true : null
E. Runtime Exception

5.1.24 Given code of Test.java file:

```java
package com.udayan.stream;

import java.util.OptionalDouble;

class MyException extends RuntimeException{}

public class Test {
    public static void main(String[] args) {
        OptionalDouble optional = OptionalDouble.empty();
        System.out.println(optional
                .orElseThrow(MyException::new));
    }
}
```

What will be the result of compiling and executing Test class?

A. null
B. An instance of NoSuchElementException is thrown at runtime
C. An instance of RuntimeException is thrown at runtime
D. An instance of MyException is thrown at runtime
E. An instance of NullPointerException is thrown at runtime
F. Compilation error

5.1.25 Given code of Test.java file:

```java
package com.udayan.stream;

import java.util.OptionalInt;

class MyException extends Exception{}

public class Test {
    public static void main(String[] args) {
        OptionalInt optional = OptionalInt.empty();
        System.out.println(optional
                .orElseThrow(MyException::new));
    }
}
```

What will be the result of compiling and executing Test class?

A. null
B. An instance of NoSuchElementException is thrown at runtime
C. An instance of RuntimeException is thrown at runtime
D. An instance of MyException is thrown at runtime
E. An instance of NullPointerException is thrown at runtime
F. Compilation error

5.1.26 Which of the following are Primitive variant of Optional class?

A. ByteOptional
B. IntOptional
C. OptionalBoolean
D. OptionalFloat
E. OptionalDouble

5.1.27 Given code of Test.java file:

```java
package com.udayan.stream;

import java.util.Optional;
import java.util.stream.Stream;

public class Test {
    public static void main(String[] args) {
        Stream<String> stream
                = Stream.of("a", "as", "an", "and");
        Optional<String> first = stream.findFirst();
        if(first.ifPresent()) {
            System.out.println(first.get());
        }
    }
}
```

What will be the result of compiling and executing Test class?

A. a

B. Any element from the stream is printed

C. Compilation error

D. Runtime Exception

5.1.28 Given code of Test.java file:

```java
package com.udayan.stream;

import java.util.Random;
import java.util.stream.IntStream;

public class Test {
    public static void main(String[] args) {
        IntStream stream = IntStream.generate(
            () -> new Random().nextInt(100)).limit(5);
        stream.filter(i -> i > 0 && i < 10)
                    .findFirst()._____;
    }
}
```

Which code snippet, when filled into the blank, allows the class to compile?

A.	`get()`
B.	`map(i -> i * i)`
C.	`forEach(System.out::println)`
D.	`ifPresent(System.out::println)`

5.1.29 Given code of Test.java file:

```java
package com.udayan.stream;

import java.util.Random;
import java.util.stream.IntStream;

public class Test {
    public static void main(String[] args) {
        IntStream stream = new Random()
                                .ints(1, 7).limit(2);
        System.out.println(stream.max().getAsInt());
    }
}
```

Above code compiles and executes successfully and generates random integers.

Which of the following is not the possible output of above code?

A. 4

B. 5

C. 6

D. 7

5.1.30 Given code of Test.java file:

```java
package com.udayan.stream;

import java.util.stream.IntStream;

public class Test {
    public static void main(String[] args) {
        IntStream.range(1, 10).forEach(System.out::print);
    }
}
```

What will be the result of compiling and executing Test class?

A. 123456789

B. 12345678910

C. 13579

D. 246810

5.1.31 Given code of Test.java file:

```java
package com.udayan.stream;

import java.util.stream.LongStream;

public class Test {
    public static void main(String[] args) {
        LongStream.iterate(0, i -> i + 2).limit(4)
                        .forEach(System.out::print);
    }
}
```

What will be the result of compiling and executing Test class?

A. 02

B. 024

C. 0246

D. 02468

5.1.32 Given code of Test.java file:

```java
package com.udayan.stream;

import java.util.stream.Stream;

class Employee {
    private String name;
    private double salary;

    public Employee(String name, double salary) {
        this.name = name;
        this.salary = salary;
    }

    public String getName() {
        return name;
    }

    public double getSalary() {
        return salary;
    }

    public String toString() {
        return "{" + name + ", " + salary + "}";
    }

    public static int salaryCompare(double d1, double d2) {
        return new Double(d2).compareTo(d1);
    }
}

public class Test {
    public static void main(String[] args) {
        Stream<Employee> employees
            = Stream.of(new Employee("Jack", 10000),
            new Employee("Lucy", 12000),
            new Employee("Tom", 7000));

        highestSalary(employees);
    }

    private static void highestSalary(
```

```
                                      Stream<Employee> emp) {
        System.out.println(emp
            .map(e -> e.getSalary())
            .max(Employee::salaryCompare));
    }
}
```

What will be the result of compiling and executing Test class?

A. Optional[10000.0]

B. Optional[12000.0]

C. Optional[7000.0]

D. Optional.empty

5.1.33 Given code of Test.java file:

```
package com.udayan.stream;

import java.util.stream.IntStream;

public class Test {
    public static void main(String[] args) {
        int sum = IntStream.rangeClosed(1,3)
                .map(i -> i * i).map(i -> i * i).sum();
        System.out.println(sum);
    }
}
```

What will be the result of compiling and executing Test class?

A. 6

B. 14

C. 98

D. None of the other options

5.1.34 Given code of Test.java file:

```java
package com.udayan.stream;

import java.util.Arrays;
import java.util.stream.Stream;

public class Test {
    public static void main(String[] args) {
        Stream<Integer> stream
                = Arrays.asList(1,2,3,4,5).stream();
        System.out.println(stream.sum());
    }
}
```

What will be the result of compiling and executing Test class?

A. 15

B. Runtime Exception

C. Compilation error

5.1.35 Given code of Test.java file:

```java
package com.udayan.stream;

import java.util.stream.Stream;

public class Test {
    public static void main(String[] args) {
        Stream<Double> stream = Stream.of(9.8, 2.3, -3.0);
        System.out.println(stream.min());
    }
}
```

What will be the result of compiling and executing Test class?

A. Compilation error

B. Runtime Exception

C. -3.0

D. 2.3

5.1.36 Given code of Test.java file:

```java
package com.udayan.stream;

import java.util.stream.LongStream;

public class Test {
    public static void main(String[] args) {
        LongStream stream = LongStream.empty();
        System.out.println(stream.average());
    }
}
```

What will be the result of compiling and executing Test class?

A. null

B. 0.0

C. OptionalDouble.empty

D. Runtime exception

5.1.37 Given code of Test.java file:

```java
package com.udayan.stream;

import java.util.Arrays;
import java.util.stream.Stream;

public class Test {
    public static void main(String[] args) {
        Stream<Integer> stream
                = Arrays.asList(1,2,3,4,5).stream();
        System.out.println(
            stream.mapToInt(i -> i).average().getAsInt());
    }
}
```

What will be the result of compiling and executing Test class?

A. 3

B. Runtime Exception

C. Compilation error

5.1.38 Given code of Test.java file:

```java
package com.udayan.stream;

import java.util.stream.IntStream;

public class Test {
    public static void main(String[] args) {
        IntStream stream = IntStream.rangeClosed(1, 20)
                            .filter(i -> i % 2 == 0);
        System.out.println(stream.summaryStatistics());
    }
}
```

Which of the following statements is true for above code?

A. On execution only sum and average data will be printed on to the console.

B. On execution only max, min and count data will be printed on to the console.

C. On execution sum, average, max, min and count data will be printed on to the console.

D. On execution a text containing @ symbol will be printed on to the console.

5.1.39 Given code of Test.java file:

```java
package com.udayan.stream;

import java.util.Arrays;
import java.util.IntSummaryStatistics;
import java.util.stream.Stream;

public class Test {
    public static void main(String[] args) {
        String text =
            "I am going to pass OCP exam in first attempt";
        Stream<String> stream =
            Arrays.stream(text.split(" "));
        IntSummaryStatistics stat =
            stream.map(s -> s.length()).summaryStatistics();
        System.out.println(stat.getMax());
    }
}
```

Which of the following needs to be done, so that output is 7?

A. No need to make any changes, on execution given code prints 7 on to the console.
B. Replace 'text.split(" ")' with 'text.split(",")'
C. Replace 'stream.map(s -> s.length())' with 'stream.mapToInt(s -> s.length())'
D. Replace 'stat.getMax()' with 'stat.getCount()'

5.1.40 Given code of Test.java file:

```java
package com.udayan.stream;

import java.util.stream.IntStream;

public class Test {
    public static void main(String[] args) {
        int res = 1;
        IntStream stream = IntStream.rangeClosed(1, 5);

        /*INSERT*/
    }
}
```

Which of the following options can replace /*INSERT*/ such that on executing Test class, 120 is printed in the output?

NOTE: 120 is the multiplication of numbers from 1 to 5. Select 2 options.

A.	System.*out*.println(stream.reduce(1, (i, j) -> i * j));
B.	System.*out*.println(stream.reduce(0, (i, j) -> i * j));
C.	System.*out*.println(stream.reduce(res, (i, j) -> i * j));
D.	System.*out*.println(stream.reduce(1, Integer::multiply));
E.	System.*out*.println(stream.reduce(0, Integer::multiply));

Java Functional Programming - Lambda & Stream Practice Tests

5.1.41 Given code of Test.java file:

```java
package com.udayan.stream;

import java.util.stream.IntStream;

public class Test {
    public static void main(String[] args) {
        int res = 1;
        IntStream stream = IntStream.rangeClosed(1, 4);

        System.out.println(stream.reduce(res++,
                                  (i, j) -> i * j));
    }
}
```

What will be the result of compiling and executing Test class?

A. 24

B. 48

C. 12

D. 6

E. Compilation error as res should be effectively final

5.1.42 Given code of Test.java file:

```java
package com.udayan.stream;

import java.util.Arrays;
import java.util.stream.Stream;

public class Test {
    public static void main(String[] args) {
        Stream<String> stream = Arrays.asList("One",
                          "Two", "Three").stream();
        System.out.println(stream.reduce(null,
                          (s1, s2) -> s1 + s2));
    }
}
```

What will be the result of compiling and executing Test class?

A. OneTwoThree

B. nullOneTwoThree

C. NullPointerException is thrown at runtime

D. OneTwoThreenull

5.1.43 Given code of Test.java file:

```java
package com.udayan.stream;

import java.util.Arrays;
import java.util.stream.Stream;

public class Test {
    public static void main(String[] args) {
        Stream<Double> stream =
                Arrays.asList(1.8, 2.2, 3.5).stream();

        /*INSERT*/
    }
}
```

Which of the following options can replace /*INSERT*/ such that on executing Test class, all the stream elements are added and result is printed on to the console? Select ALL that apply.

A.	`System.out.println(stream.reduce(0.0, (d1, d2) -> d1 + d2));`
B.	`System.out.println(stream.reduce(0.0, Double::sum));`
C.	`System.out.println(stream.reduce(0, (d1, d2) -> d1 + d2));`
D.	`System.out.println(stream.reduce(0, Double::sum));`
E.	`System.out.println(stream.sum());`

5.1.44 Given code of Test.java file:

```java
package com.udayan.stream;

import java.util.Arrays;
import java.util.stream.Stream;

public class Test {
    public static void main(String[] args) {
        Stream<Double> stream =
            Arrays.asList(1.8, 2.2, 3.5).stream();
        System.out.println(stream.reduce(
                (d1, d2) -> d1 + d2)); //Line 9
    }
}
```

What will be the result of compiling and executing Test class?

A. Optional[7.5]

B. 7.5

C. Line 9 causes Compilation error

5.1.45 Given code of Test.java file:

```java
package com.udayan.stream;

import java.util.Arrays;

public class Test {
    public static void main(String[] args) {
        String [] names = {"Peter", "bonita", "John"};
        Arrays.stream(names).sorted((s1, s2)
                -> s1.compareToIgnoreCase(s2))
            .forEach(System.out::println);
    }
}
```

What will be the result of compiling and executing Test class?

A.	Peter bonita John	B.	John bonita Peter
C.	bonita John Peter	D.	John Peter bonita

5.1.46 Given code of Test.java file:

```java
package com.udayan.stream;

import java.util.Comparator;
import java.util.stream.Stream;

public class Test {
    public static void main(String[] args) {
        Comparator<Integer> comp
                = (i1, i2) -> i2.compareTo(i1);
        Stream<Integer> stream
                = Stream.of(55, 23, -9, 8, 42);
        stream.sorted(comp.reversed())
                .forEach(i -> System.out.print(i + " "));
    }
}
```

What will be the result of compiling and executing Test class?

A. 55 42 23 8 -9

B. -9 8 23 42 55

C. 55 23 -9 8 42

D. 42 8 -9 23 55

5.1.47 Given code of Test.java file:

```java
package com.udayan.stream;

import java.util.stream.Stream;

public class Test {
    public static void main(String[] args) {
        Stream<String> stream
            = Stream.of("d", "cc", "bbb", "aaaa");
        stream.sorted().forEach(System.out::println);
    }
}
```

Which of the following needs to be done, so that output is:

d

cc

bbb

aaaa

A. No need to make any changes, on execution given code prints expected result.

B. Replace 'stream.sorted()' with 'stream.sorted((s1,s2) -> s1.length() - s2.length())'

C. Replace 'stream.sorted()' with 'stream.sorted((s1,s2) -> s2.length() - s1.length())'

5.1.48 Given code of Test.java file:

```java
package com.udayan.stream;

import java.util.Comparator;
import java.util.stream.Stream;

public class Test {
    public static void main(String[] args) {
        Stream<String> stream = Stream.of("d", "a",
                        "mm", "bb", "zzz", "www");
        Comparator<String> lengthComp =
                (s1, s2) -> s1.length() - s2.length();
        stream.sorted(lengthComp)
                        .forEach(System.out::println);
    }
}
```

Which of the following needs to be done, so that output is:
a
d
bb
mm
www
zzz

A. No need to make any changes, on execution given code prints expected result.

B. Replace 'stream.sorted(lengthComp)' with
   'stream.sorted(lengthComp.thenComparing(String::compareTo))'

C. Replace 'stream.sorted(lengthComp)' with 'stream.sorted(lengthComp.reversed())'

5.1.49 Given code of Test.java file:

```java
package com.udayan.stream;

import java.util.Arrays;
import java.util.stream.Stream;

public class Test {
    public static void main(String[] args) {
        String [] arr1 =
            {"Virat", "Rohit", "Shikhar", "Dhoni"};
        String [] arr2 =
            {"Bumrah", "Pandya", "Sami"};
        String [] arr3 = {};

        Stream<String[]> stream =
                    Stream.of(arr1, arr2, arr3);
        stream.flatMap(s -> Arrays.stream(s)).sorted()
            .forEach(s -> System.out.print(s + " "));
    }
}
```

What will be the result of compiling and executing Test class?

A. Virat Rohit Shikhar Dhoni Bumrah Pandya Sami
B. Virat Rohit Shikhar Dhoni Bumrah Pandya Sami null
C. null Bumrah Dhoni Pandya Rohit Sami Shikhar Virat
D. Bumrah Dhoni Pandya Rohit Sami Shikhar Virat
E. Bumrah Dhoni Pandya Rohit Sami Shikhar Virat null

5.1.50 Given code of Test.java file:

```java
package com.udayan.stream;

import java.util.stream.Stream;

public class Test {
    public static void main(String[] args) {
        Stream<String> stream = Stream.of("ocp");
        stream._____(s -> s.chars())
            .forEach(i -> System.out.print((char)i));
    }
}
```

Which code snippet, when filled into the blank, allows the class to compile?

A. flatMap

B. flatMapToInt

C. flatMapToDouble

D. flatMapToLong

5.2 Answers of Practice Test - 5 with Explanation

5.1.1 Answer: D

Reason:
Stream.of() returns blank stream. As Type of stream is specified, stream is of 'Stream<StringBuilder>', each element of the stream is considered to be of 'StringBuilder' type.

map method in this case accepts 'Function<? super StringBuilder, ? extends StringBuilder>'.

In Lambda expression 's -> s.reverse()', s is of StringBuilder type and hence no compilation error.

As stream is blank, hence map and forEach methods are not executed even once. Program executes fine but nothing is printed on to the console.

5.1.2 Answer: A

Reason:
Stream.of() returns blank stream. As Type of stream is not specified, stream is of 'Stream<Object>', each element of the stream is considered to be of 'Object' type.

map method in this case accepts 'Function<? super Object, ? extends R>'.

There is no 'reverse()' method in Object class and hence lambda expression causes compilation failure.

5.1.3 Answer: D

Reason:
Streams are lazily evaluated, which means for finite streams, if terminal operations such as: forEach, count, toArray, reduce, collect, findFirst, findAny, anyMatch, allMatch, sum, min, max, average etc. are not present, the given stream pipeline is not evaluated and hence peek() method doesn't print anything on to the console.

5.1.4   Answer: B

Reason:
String class implements CharSequence interface and it has a default method chars() which returns IntStream object.

forEach, count, toArray, reduce, collect, findFirst, findAny, anyMatch, allMatch, sum, min, max, average etc. are considered as terminal operations.

Once the terminal operation is complete, all the elements of the stream are considered as used. Any attempt to use the stream again causes IllegalStateException.

In this example, count() is used after using forEach() method and hence IllegalStateException is thrown.

5.1.5   Answer: B

Reason:
count() is a terminal method for finite stream, hence peek(System.out::println) is executed for all the 3 elements of the stream.

count() method returns long value but it is not used.

5.1.6   Answer: C

Reason:
Method signatures:
boolean anyMatch(Predicate<? super T>) : Returns true if any of the stream element matches the given Predicate. If stream is empty, it returns false and predicate is not evaluated.

boolean allMatch(Predicate<? super T>) : Returns true if all the stream elements match the given Predicate. If stream is empty, it returns true and predicate is not evaluated.

boolean noneMatch(Predicate<? super T>) : Returns true if none of the stream element matches the given Predicate. If stream is empty, it returns true and predicate is not evaluated.

In this case, as stream is empty anyMatch returns false whereas allMatch and noneMatch both returns true.

5.1.7   Answer: B

Reason:
Method signatures:
boolean anyMatch(Predicate<? super T>) : Returns true if any of the stream element matches the given Predicate. If stream is empty, it returns false and predicate is not evaluated.

boolean allMatch(Predicate<? super T>) : Returns true if all the stream elements match the given Predicate. If stream is empty, it returns true and predicate is not evaluated.

boolean noneMatch(Predicate<? super T>) : Returns true if none of the stream element matches the given Predicate. If stream is empty, it returns true and predicate is not evaluated.

In the given code,
Stream.generate(() -> new Double("1.0")).limit(10); => returns a Stream<Double> containing 10 elements and each element is 1.0.

stream.filter(d -> d > 2) => returns an empty stream as given predicate is not true for even 1 element.

allMatch method, when invoked on empty stream, returns true.

5.1.8   Answer: A

Reason:
stream => {1, 2, 3, 4, 5, ... }. It is an infinite stream.
Predicate 'i -> i > 1' returns true for any Integer greater than 1.
As 2 > 1, so true is printed and operation is terminated. Code doesn't run infinitely.

NOTE: 'stream.allMatch(i -> i > 1)' returns false as 1st element of the stream (1) returns false for the predicate and 'stream.noneMatch(i -> i > 1)' returns false as 2nd element of the stream (2) returns true for the predicate.

5.1.9 Answer: C

Reason:
Method signature for anyMatch method:
boolean anyMatch(Predicate<? super T>) : Returns true if any of the stream element matches the given Predicate. If stream is empty, it returns false and predicate is not evaluated.

As given stream is empty, hence predicate is not evaluated and nothing is printed on to the console.

5.1.10 Answer: B

Reason:
Method signature for anyMatch method:
boolean anyMatch(Predicate<? super T>) : Returns true if any of the stream element matches the given Predicate. If stream is empty, it returns false and predicate is not evaluated.

ref is a local variable and it is used within lambda expression. ++ref causes compilation failure as variable ref should be effectively final.

5.1.11 Answer: B

Reason:
Stream.of("red", "green", "blue", "yellow") => ["red", "green", "blue", "yellow"].

sorted() => ["blue", "green", "red", "yellow"].

findFirst() => ["blue"]. findFirst returns Optional<String> object.

5.1.12 Answer: C

Reason:
Stream.generate(() -> new Double("1.0")); generates an infinite stream of Double, whose elements are 1.0.

stream.sorted() is an intermediate operation and needs all the elements to be available for sorting. As all the elements of infinite stream are never available, hence sorted() method never completes. So among all the available option, correct option is: 'Nothing is printed and program runs infinitely.'

5.1.13 Answer: D

Reason:
There is no stream() method available in Map interface and hence map.stream() causes compilation error.

Though you can first get either entrySet or keySet or values and then invoke stream() method.

For example, below code prints all the key value pairs available in the map:
map.entrySet().stream().forEach(x -> System.out.println(x.getKey() + ":" + x.getValue()));

5.1.14 Answer: A

Reason:
findFirst() will never return empty Optional if stream is not empty. So no exception for get() method.

Also list and stream are not connected, which means operations done on stream doesn't affect the source, in this case list.

list.get(2) will print 'X' on to the console.

5.1.15 Answer: B

Reason:
Optional<T> is a final class and overrides toString() method:

```
public String toString() {
   return value != null
      ? String.format("Optional[%s]", value)
      : "Optional.empty";
}
```

In the question, Optional is of Integer type and Integer class overrides toString() method, so output is: Optional[10]

5.1.16 Answer: D

Reason:
If null argument is passed to of method, then NullPointerException is thrown at runtime.

5.1.17 Answer: A

Reason:
ofNullable method creates an empty Optional object if passed argument is null.

Optional.empty is printed on to the console for empty Optional.

5.1.18 Answer: C

Reason:
Stream.of() creates an empty stream.
stream.findFirst(); => returns an empty Optional. Hence, orElse method is executed and prints -1 on to the console.

Java Functional Programming - Lambda & Stream Practice Tests

5.1.19 Answer: C

Reason:
Optional.of(null); throws NullPointerException as null arguments is passed.

You can use 'Optional.ofNullable(null);' to create an empty optional.

5.1.20 Answer: B

Reason:
stream => ["and", "Or", "not", "Equals", "unary", "binary"].

Test::isFirstCharVowel is the predicate, to invoke negate() method, it needs to be type-casted to 'Predicate<String>'.

stream.filter(((Predicate<String>)Test::isFirstCharVowel).negate()) => ["not", "binary"].

findFirst() => Optional<String> object containing "not".

optional.get() => "not".

5.1.21 Answer: A,E

Reason:
findAny() may return any element from the stream and as stream is not parallel, it will most likely return first element from the sorted stream, which is -10. But this is not the guaranteed result.
As this stream has 3 elements, hence -1 will never get printed on to the console.

5.1.22 Answer: B

Reason:
stream => [{2018-1-1}, {2018-1-1}].
stream.distinct() => [{2018-1-1}].
findAny() => Optional[{2018-1-1}].

optional.isPresent() => true. isPresent method returns true if optional is not empty otherwise false.
optional.get() => Returns LocalDate object {2018-1-1}, toString() method of LocalDate class pads 0 to single digit month and day.

'true : 2018-01-01' is printed on to the console.

NOTE: In real world projects, it is advisable to to check using isPresent() method before using the get() method.
if(optional.isPresent()) {
   System.out.println(optional.get());
}

5.1.23 Answer: E

Reason:
In this case, value variable inside Optional instance is null.

optional.isPresent() => false. isPresent method returns true if optional is not empty otherwise false.

If value variable inside Optional instance is null (empty optional), then NoSuchElementException is thrown at runtime.

In real world projects, it is advisable to to check using isPresent() method before using the get() method.
if(optional.isPresent()) {
   System.out.println(optional.getAsLong());
}

NOTE: There are 3 primitive equivalents of Optional<T> interface available. Remember their similarity with Optional<T> class.

Optional<T>:
Optional<T> empty(),
T get(),
boolean isPresent(),

Optional<T> of(T),
void ifPresent(Consumer<? super T>),
T orElse(T),
T orElseGet(Supplier<? extends T>),
T orElseThrow(Supplier<? extends X>),
Optional<T> filter(Predicate<? super T>),
Optional<U> map(Function<? super T, ? extends U>),
Optional<U> flatMap(Function<? super T, Optional<U>>).

OptionalInt:
OptionalInt empty(),
int getAsInt(),
boolean isPresent(),
OptionalInt of(int),
void ifPresent(IntConsumer),
int orElse(int),
orElseGet(IntSupplier),
int orElseThrow(Supplier<X>).
[filter, map and faltMap methods are not available in primitive type].

OptionalLong:
OptionalLong empty(),
long getAsLong(),
boolean isPresent(),
OptionalLong of(long),
void ifPresent(LongConsumer),
long orElse(long),
long orElseGet(LongSupplier),
long orElseThrow(Supplier<X>).
[filter, map and faltMap methods are not available in primitive type].

OptionalDouble:
OptionalDouble empty(),
double getAsDouble(),
boolean isPresent(),
OptionalDouble of(double),
void ifPresent(DoubleConsumer),

double orElse(double),
double orElseGet(DoubleSupplier),
double orElseThrow(Supplier<X>).
[filter, map and faltMap methods are not available in primitive type].

5.1.24 Answer: D

Reason:
orElseThrow throws the instance of provided Exception if optional is empty.

In this case optional is an empty OptionalDouble, hence an instance of MyException is thrown at runtime.

5.1.25 Answer: F

Reason:
MyException is a checked exception, so 'handle or declare' rule must be followed.

'orElseThrow(MyException::new)' can throw checked exception at runtime, so it must be surrounded by a try-catch block or main method should declare proper throws clause.

5.1.26 Answer: E

Reason:
Only 3 primitive variants available: OptionalDouble, OptionalInt and OptionalLong.

5.1.27 Answer: C

Reason:
Method isPresent() returns boolean whereas method ifPresent accepts a Consumer parameter. 'first.ifPresent()' causes compilation failure.

5.1.28 Answer: D

Reason:
It is very simple as you don't have to worry about return type of the code snippet. stream is of IntStream type. Even method filter returns instance of IntStream type. findFirst() returns an OptionalInt as it is called on IntStream.

Of all the given options, OptionalInt has 'ifPresent' method only. Hence correct answer is: 'ifPresent(System.out::println)'.

5.1.29 Answer: D

Reason:
new Random().ints(start, end) => start is inclusive and end is exclusive. So this code generates random integers between 1 and 6. All the 6 integers from 1 to 6 are possible.

Above code will never generate 7.

5.1.30 Answer: A

Reason:
IntStream.range(int start, int end) => start is inclusive and end is exclusive and incremental step is 1. So, stream consists of value from 1 to 9 and these values are printed by forEach method.

NOTE: For IntStream.rangeClosed(int start, int end), both start and end are inclusive.

5.1.31 Answer: C

Reason:
LongStream.iterate(long seed, LongUnaryOperator f) => 'seed' is the initial element and 'f' is a function to be applied to the previous element to produce a new element.

LongUnaryOperator is a functional interface and has method 'long applyAsLong(long operand);'. This means lambda expression should accept long parameter and return long value.
'i -> i + 2' is the correct lambda expression.

LongStream.iterate(0, i -> i + 2) => This results in an infinite stream consisting of elements [0,2,4,6,8,10,12,...]

limit(4) => Returns a stream consisting of 4 elements [0,2,4,6] from the given stream.
Hence, the output is: 0246

5.1.32 Answer: C

Reason:
In real exam, don't predict the output by just looking at the method name.

It is expected that highestSalary(...) method will print 'Optional[12000.0]' on to the console but if you closely check the definition of Employee.salaryCompare(...) method you will note that it helps to sort the salary in descending order and not ascending order.

Rest of the logic is pretty simple.
emp => [{"Jack", 10000.0}, {"Lucy", 12000.0}, {"Tom", 7000.0}].

emp.map(e -> e.getSalary()) => [10000.0, 12000.0, 7000.0].

max(Employee::salaryCompare) => Optional[7000].

NOTE: There are 3 methods in Stream interface, which returns Optional<T> type:
1. Optional<T> max(Comparator<? super T> comparator);
2. Optional<T> min(Comparator<? super T> comparator);
3. Optional<T> reduce(BinaryOperator<T> accumulator);

5.1.33 Answer: C

Reason:
IntStream.rangeClosed(int start, int end) => Returns a sequential stream from start to end, both inclusive and with a step of 1.

IntStream.map(IntUnaryOperator) => Returns a stream consisting of the results of applying the given function to the elements of this stream.

IntStream.rangeClosed(1,3) => [1,2,3].

map(i -> i * i) => [1,4,9].

map(i -> i * i) => [1,16,81].

sum() => 1+16+81 = 98.

5.1.34 Answer: C

Reason:
Generic Stream<T> interface has following methods:
Optional<T> min(Comparator<? super T> comparator);
Optional<T> max(Comparator<? super T> comparator);

Primitive Stream interfaces (IntStream, LongStream & DoubleStream) has methods min(), max(), sum(), average() and summaryStatistics().

In this case, as stream is a generic interface, hence stream.sum() causes compilation error.

5.1.35 Answer: A

Reason:
stream is of Stream<Double> type, which is a generic stream and not primitive stream. There is no min() method available in generic stream interface, Stream<T> and hence, 'stream.min()' causes compilation error.

Generic Stream<T> interface has following methods:

Optional<T> min(Comparator<? super T> comparator);
Optional<T> max(Comparator<? super T> comparator);

To calculate min for generic Stream, pass the Comparator as argument:
stream.min(Double::compareTo), but note it will return an instance of Optional<Double> type.

5.1.36 Answer: C

Reason:
average() method in IntStream, LongStream and DoubleStream returns OptionalDouble.

As stream is an empty stream, hence 'stream.average()' returns an empty optional.

OptionalDouble.empty is printed on to the console for empty Optional.

5.1.37 Answer: C

Reason:
stream.mapToInt(i -> i) => returns an instance of IntStream.

average() method of all the 3 primitive streams (IntStream, LongStream & DoubleStream) return an instance of OptionalDouble. OptionalDouble has getAsDouble() method and not getAsInt() method.

5.1.38 Answer: C

Reason:
There are 3 summary statistics methods available in JDK 8: IntSummaryStatistics, LongSummaryStatistics & DoubleSummaryStatistics.

summaryStatistics() method in IntStream class returns an instance of IntSummaryStatistics.
summaryStatistics() method in LongStream class returns an instance of LongSummaryStatistics.
summaryStatistics() method in DoubleStream class returns an instance of DoubleSummaryStatistics.

The 3 summary statistics classes override toString() method to print the data about count, sum, min, average and max.

All the 3 summary statistics classes have methods to extract specific stat as well: getCount(), getSum(), getMin(), getMax() and getAverage().

Summary Statistics are really useful if you want multiple stats, say for example you want to find both min and max. As min and max are terminal operation for finite stream so after using one operation stream gets closed and not possible to use the same stream for other terminal operations.

5.1.39 Answer: C

Reason:
text.split(" ") => {"I", "am", "going", "to", "pass", "OCP", "exam", "in", "first", "attempt"}.
Arrays.stream(text.split(" ")); => ["I", "am", "going", "to", "pass", "OCP", "exam", "in", "first", "attempt"]. Stream<String> instance is returned.
stream.map(s -> s.length()) => [1, 2, 5, 2, 4, 3, 4, 2, 5, 7]. Stream<Integer> is returned.

summaryStatistics() method is declared in IntStream, LongStream and DoubleStream interfaces but not declared in Stream<Integer> interface and hence 'stream.map(s -> s.length()).summaryStatistics();' causes compilation failure.

Out of the given options, replacing 'stream.map(s -> s.length())' with 'stream.mapToInt(s -> s.length())' will correctly return an instance of IntStream and hence summaryStatistics() method can easily be invoked.

As you had to select only one option, so you can stop here. No need to validate other options. I am explaining other options just for knowledge purpose.

stat.getCount() will return 10 so not a correct option.

text.split(" ") delimits the text on the basis of single space. text.split(",") will delimit it on the basis of comma but as no comma is present in the given text, hence whole text will be returned and stat.getMax() will print 44.

5.1.40 Answer: A, C

Reason:
Integer class doesn't have 'multiply' method, hence options containing 'Integer::multiply' will cause compilation failure.

To understand, 'stream.reduce(1, (i, j) -> i * j)' can be written as:

```
int result = 1;
for (int element : stream) {
   result = op.applyAsInt(result, element);
}
return result;
```

Above code is just for understanding purpose, you can't iterate a stream using given loop.

Note: 'op' in above code is of IntBinaryOperator and target type of given lambda expression.

Check IntPipeline class which implements IntStream for the details of reduce method.

If 1st argument of reduce is 0, then overall result will be zero.

'stream.reduce(1, (i, j) -> i * j)' and 'stream.reduce(res, (i, j) -> i * j)' are correct options.

5.1.41 Answer: A

Reason:
IntStream.rangeClosed(1, 4); => [1, 2, 3, 4]

To understand, 'stream.reduce(res++, (i, j) -> i * j)' can be somewhat written as:

```
int result = res++;
for (int element : stream) {
   result = accumulator.applyAsInt(result, element);
}
```

return result;

Above code is just for understanding purpose, you can't iterate a stream using given loop.

result will be initialized to 1 and after that res will be incremented to 2. But value of 'result' is used and not 'res'.
Hence output will be result of '1 * 1 * 2 * 3 * 4', which is 24.

5.1.42 Answer: B

Reason:
Given reduce method concatenates null + "One" + "Two" + "Three" and hence the output is: 'nullOneTwoThree'.

To concatenate just the stream contents, use below code:
stream.reduce("", (s1, s2) -> s1 + s2)
OR
stream.reduce((s1, s2) -> s1 + s2).get()

5.1.43 Answer: A,B

Reason:
'stream.reduce(0.0, (d1, d2) -> d1 + d2)' and 'stream.reduce(0.0, Double::sum)' are exactly same and adds all the stream contents.

stream.sum() causes compilation error as sum() method is declared only in primitive streams (IntStream, LongStream and DoubleStream) but not in generic stream, Stream<T>.

reduce method parameters are (Double, BinaryOperator).
0 (int literal) cannot be converted to Double and hence compilation error for 'stream.reduce(0, (d1, d2) -> d1 + d2)' and 'stream.reduce(0, Double::sum)'.

You can easily verify this by writing below code:
public class Test {
    public static void main(String[] args) {

```
        print(0); //Compilation error as int can't be converted to Double
    }

    private static void print(Double d) {
        System.out.println(d);
    }
}
```

5.1.44   Answer: A

Reason:
'stream.reduce((d1, d2) -> d1 + d2)' returns 'Optional<Double>' type whereas 'stream.reduce(0.0, (d1, d2) -> d1 + d2)' returns 'Double'.

5.1.45   Answer: C

Reason:
In this example, Stream<String> is used. sorted method accepts Comparator<? super String> type.

compareToIgnoreCase is defined in String class and it compares the text by in case-insensitive manner. Even though 'b' is in lower case it is printed first, followed by 'J' and 'P'.

5.1.46   Answer: B

Reason:
'(i1, i2) -> i2.compareTo(i1)' helps to sort in descending order. Code is: 'i2.compareTo(i1)' and not 'i1.compareTo(i2)'.

comp.reversed() returns a Comparator for sorting in ascending order. Hence, the output is: '-9 8 23 42 55 '.

5.1.47 Answer: B

Reason:
Given code sorts the stream in natural order (a appears before b, b appears before c and so on).

To get the expected output, stream should be sorted in ascending order of length of the string. Replacing 'stream.sorted()' with 'stream.sorted((s1,s2) -> s1.length() - s2.length())' will do the trick.

5.1.48 Answer: B

Reason:
Current code displays below output:
d
a
mm
bb
zzz
www

if string's length is same, then insertion order is preserved.

Requirement is to sort the stream in ascending order of length of the string and if length is same, then sort on natural order.

lengthComp is for sorting the string on the basis of length, thenComparing default method of Comparator interface allows to pass 2nd level of Comparator.
Hence replacing 'stream.sorted()' with 'stream.sorted(lengthComp.thenComparing(String::compareTo))' will do the trick.

stream.sorted(lengthComp.reversed()) will simply reversed the order, which means longest string will be printed first, but this is not expected.

5.1.49   Answer: D

Reason:
stream is not of Stream<String> type rather it is of Stream<String[]> type.
flatMap method combines all the non-empty streams and returns an instance of Stream<String> containing the individual elements from non-empty stream.

stream => [{"Virat", "Rohit", "Shikhar", "Dhoni"}, {"Bumrah", "Pandya", "Sami"}, {}].
stream.flatMap(s -> Arrays.stream(s)) => ["Virat", "Rohit", "Shikhar", "Dhoni", "Bumrah", "Pandya", "Sami"].
sorted() => ["Bumrah", "Dhoni", "Pandya", "Rohit", "Sami", "Shikhar", "Virat"].

5.1.50   Answer: B

Reason:
s -> s.chars() is of IntStream type as chars() method returns instance of IntStream type.

All 4 are valid method names but each specify different parameters. Only faltMapToInt can accept argument of IntStream type.

6 Practice Test-6
6.1 This practice test covers questions on:
- Method stream() of Collection interface
- Save results to a collection using the collect method and group/partition data using the Collectors class
- forEach(Consumer) method of Iterator<T> interface
- Convert arrays and collections to streams
- stream() and parallelStream() methods of Collection interface
- parallel() and sequential() method of Stream interface
- Behavior of various methods such as forEach, reduce, forEachOrdered, findFirst with parallel streams

6.1.1 Given code of Test.java file:

```java
package com.udayan.stream;

import java.util.*;

public class Test {
    public static void main(String[] args) {
        int i = 2000;
        List<Integer> list = new ArrayList<>();
        list.add(1000);
        list.add(i);
        list.add(3000);

        /*INSERT*/
    }
}
```

Which of the following statements, if used to replace /*INSERT*/, will print following on to the console:
1000
2000
3000

Select ALL that apply.

A. `list.forEach(System.out::print);`

B. `list.forEach(System.out::println);`

C. `list.forEach(i -> System.out.println(i));`

D. `list.forEach(s -> System.out.println(s));`

6.1.2 Given code of Test.java file:

```java
package com.udayan.stream;

import java.util.*;

class Employee {
    private String name;
    private double salary;

    public Employee(String name, double salary) {
        this.name = name;
        this.salary = salary;
    }

    public String getName() {
        return name;
    }

    public double getSalary() {
        return salary;
    }

    public void setSalary(double salary) {
        this.salary = salary;
    }

    public String toString() {
        return "{" + name + ", " + salary + "}";
    }
}

public class Test {
    public static void main(String[] args) {
        List<Employee> employees = Arrays.asList(
                new Employee("Jack", 10000),
                new Employee("Lucy", 12000));
        employees.forEach(e -> e.setSalary(
                e.getSalary() + (e.getSalary() * .2)));
        employees.forEach(System.out::println);
    }
}
```

What will be the result of compiling and executing Test class?

A.	{Jack, 12000.0} {Lucy, 14400.0}	B.	{Jack, 12000} {Lucy, 14400}
C.	{Jack, 10000.0} {Lucy, 12000.0}	D.	{Jack, 10000} {Lucy, 12000}

6.1.3 Given code of Test.java file:

```java
package com.udayan.stream;

import java.util.Arrays;

public class Test {
    public static void main(String[] args) {
        String [] cities = {"Seoul", "Tokyo", "Paris",
                "London", "Hong Kong", "Singapore"};
        Arrays.stream(cities)
            .sorted((s1,s2) -> s2.compareTo(s1))
            .forEach(System.out::println);
    }
}
```

What will be the result of compiling and executing Test class?

A.	Seoul Tokyo Paris London Hong Kong Singapore	B.	Hong Kong London Paris Seoul Singapore Tokyo
C.	Tokyo Singapore Seoul Paris London Hong Kong	D.	Compilation error

6.1.4 Given code of Test.java file:

```java
package com.udayan.stream;

import java.util.Arrays;
import java.util.List;

public class Test {
    public static void main(String[] args) {
        List<String> list = Arrays.asList("A", "A",
                                "b", "B", "c", "c");
        list.stream().distinct()
                .forEach(System.out::print);
    }
}
```

What will be the result of compiling and executing Test class?

A. AAbBcc
B. AbBc
C. ABbc
D. Abc
E. ABc

6.1.5 Given code of Test.java file:

```java
package com.udayan.stream;

import java.util.ArrayList;
import java.util.List;

public class Test {
    public static void main(String[] args) {
        List<StringBuilder> list = new ArrayList<>();
        list.add(new StringBuilder("abc"));
        list.add(new StringBuilder("xyz"));
        list.stream().map(x -> x.reverse());
        System.out.println(list);
    }
}
```

What will be the result of compiling and executing Test class?

A. [cba, zyx]
B. [abc, xyz]
C. Compilation error
D. Runtime Exception

6.1.6 Given code of Test.java file:

```java
package com.udayan.stream;

public class Test {
    private static boolean isDirection(int ch) {
        switch(ch) {
            case 'N':
            case 'E':
            case 'W':
            case 'S':
                return true;
        }
        return false;
    }

    public static void main(String[] args) {
        String str = "North East West South";
        str.chars().filter(Test::isDirection)
            .forEach(c -> System.out.print((char)c));
    }
}
```

What will be the result of compiling and executing Test class?

A. orth ast est outh
B. N E W S
C. NEWS
D. None of the other options

6.1.7 Given code of Test.java file:

```java
package com.udayan.stream;

import java.util.ArrayList;
import java.util.Arrays;
import java.util.List;

public class Test {
    public static void main(String[] args) {
        List<Integer> list = new ArrayList<>(
            Arrays.asList(1,2,3,4,5,6,7,8,9,10));
        list.removeIf(i -> i % 2 == 1);
        System.out.println(list);
    }
}
```

What will be the result of compiling and executing Test class?

A. Compilation Error
B. Runtime Exception
C. [2, 4, 6, 8, 10]
D. [1, 3, 5, 7, 9]

6.1.8 Given code of Test.java file:

```java
package com.udayan.stream;

import java.util.List;
import java.util.stream.Collectors;
import java.util.stream.Stream;

public class Test {
    public static void main(String[] args) {
        Stream<String> stream = Stream.of("java",
                            "python", "c", "c++");
        List<String> list
            = stream.sorted().collect(Collectors.toList());
        System.out.println(list);
    }
}
```

What will be the result of compiling and executing Test class?

A. [c++, c, java, python]

B. [python, java, c++, c]

C. [c, c++, java, python]

D. [java, python, c, c++]

6.1.9 Given code of Test.java file:

```java
package com.udayan.stream;

import java.util.Set;
import java.util.stream.Collectors;
import java.util.stream.Stream;

public class Test {
    public static void main(String[] args) {
        Stream<String> stream = Stream.of("java",
            "python", "c", "c++", "java", "python");
        Set<String> set =
            stream.collect(Collectors.toSet());
        System.out.println(set.size());
    }
}
```

What will be the result of compiling and executing Test class?

A. 6

B. 5

C. 4

D. 0

6.1.10 Given code of Test.java file:

```java
package com.udayan.stream;

import java.util.Set;
import java.util.TreeSet;
import java.util.stream.Collectors;
import java.util.stream.Stream;

public class Test {
    public static void main(String[] args) {
        Stream<String> stream = Stream.of("java",
            "python", "c","c++", "java", "python");
        Set<String> set = stream.collect(
            Collectors.toCollection(TreeSet::new));
        System.out.println(set);
    }
}
```

What will be the result of compiling and executing Test class?

A. [c, c++, java, python]

B. [c++, c, java, python]

C. [java, python, c, c++]

D. Order of elements can't be predicted in the output.

6.1.11 Given code of Test.java file:

```java
package com.udayan.stream;

import java.util.Map;
import java.util.TreeMap;
import java.util.function.Function;
import java.util.stream.Collectors;
import java.util.stream.Stream;

class Person {
    int id;
    String name;
    Person(int id, String name) {
        this.id = id;
        this.name = name;
    }
    public String toString() {
        return "{" + id + ", " + name + "}";
    }

    public boolean equals(Object obj) {
        if(obj instanceof Person) {
            Person p = (Person) obj;
            return this.id == p.id;
        }
        return false;
    }

    public int hashCode() {
        return new Integer(this.id).hashCode();
    }
}

public class Test {
    public static void main(String[] args) {
        Person p1 = new Person(1010, "Sean");
        Person p2 = new Person(2843, "Rob");
        Person p3 = new Person(1111, "Lucy");

        Stream<Person> stream = Stream.of(p1, p2, p3);
        Map<Integer, Person> map
                = stream.collect(/*INSERT*/);
        System.out.println(map.size());
```

        }
}

Which of the following statements can replace /*INSERT*/ such that output is 3?
1. `Collectors.toMap(p -> p.id, Function.identity())`
2. `Collectors.toMap(p -> p.id, p -> p)`
3. `Collectors.toCollection(TreeMap::new)`

A. Only 1

B. Only 2

C. Only 3

D. Both 1 & 2

E. Both 2 & 3

F. All 1, 2 & 3

6.1.12 Given code of Test.java file:

```java
package com.udayan.stream;

import java.util.List;
import java.util.Map;
import java.util.stream.Collectors;
import java.util.stream.Stream;

class Certification {
    String studId;
    String test;
    int marks;

    Certification(String studId, String test, int marks) {
        this.studId = studId;
        this.test = test;
        this.marks = marks;
    }

    public String toString() {
        return "{" + studId + ", " + test
                    + ", " + marks + "}";
    }

    public String getStudId() {
```

```java
            return studId;
        }

        public String getTest() {
            return test;
        }

        public int getMarks() {
            return marks;
        }
    }

    public class Test {
        public static void main(String[] args) {
            Certification c1 =
                new Certification("S001", "OCA", 87);
            Certification c2 =
                new Certification("S002", "OCA", 82);
            Certification c3 =
                new Certification("S001", "OCP", 79);
            Certification c4 =
                new Certification("S002", "OCP", 89);
            Certification c5 =
                new Certification("S003", "OCA", 60);
            Certification c6 =
                new Certification("S004", "OCA", 88);

            Stream<Certification> stream
                = Stream.of(c1, c2, c3, c4, c5, c6);
            Map<Boolean, List<Certification>> map =
                stream.collect(Collectors.
                    partitioningBy(s -> s.equals("OCA")));
            System.out.println(map.get(true));
        }
    }
```

What will be the result of compiling and executing Test class?

A. [{S001, OCA, 87}, {S002, OCA, 82}, {S003, OCA, 60}, {S004, OCA, 88}]

B. []

C. [{S001, OCA, 87}, {S002, OCA, 82}, {S001, OCP, 79}, {S002, OCP, 89}, {S003, OCA, 60}, {S004, OCA, 88}]

D. [{S001, OCP, 79}, {S002, OCP, 89}]

6.1.13 Given code of Test.java file:

```java
package com.udayan.stream;

import java.util.List;
import java.util.Map;
import java.util.stream.Collectors;
import java.util.stream.Stream;

class Certification {
    String studId;
    String test;
    int marks;

    Certification(String studId, String test, int marks) {
        this.studId = studId;
        this.test = test;
        this.marks = marks;
    }

    public String toString() {
        return "{" + studId + ", " + test + ", "
                                + marks + "}";
    }

    public String getStudId() {
        return studId;
    }

    public String getTest() {
        return test;
    }

    public int getMarks() {
        return marks;
    }
}

public class Test {
    public static void main(String[] args) {
        Certification c1 =
            new Certification("S001", "OCA", 87);
        Certification c2 =
            new Certification("S002", "OCA", 82);
        Certification c3 =
```

```java
            new Certification("S001", "OCP", 79);
        Certification c4 =
            new Certification("S002", "OCP", 89);
        Certification c5 =
            new Certification("S003", "OCA", 60);
        Certification c6 =
            new Certification("S004", "OCA", 88);

        Stream<Certification> stream
            = Stream.of(c1, c2, c3, c4, c5, c6);
        Map<String, List<Certification>> map =
            stream.collect(Collectors.groupingBy(
                        Certification::getTest));
        System.out.println(map.get("OCP"));
    }
}
```

What will be the result of compiling and executing Test class?

A. [{S001, OCA, 87}, {S002, OCA, 82}, {S003, OCA, 60}, {S004, OCA, 88}]

B. []

C. [{S001, OCA, 87}, {S002, OCA, 82}, {S001, OCP, 79}, {S002, OCP, 89}, {S003, OCA, 60}, {S004, OCA, 88}]

D. [{S001, OCP, 79}, {S002, OCP, 89}]

6.1.14 Given code of Test.java file:

```java
package com.udayan.stream;

import java.util.stream.IntStream;

public class Test {
    public static void main(String[] args) {
        IntStream.rangeClosed(1, 10).parallel()
            .forEach(System.out::println);
    }
}
```

What will be the result of compiling and executing Test class?

A. It will print numbers from 1 to 10 in ascending order.

B. It will print numbers form 1 to 10 in descending order.

C. It will print numbers form 1 to 10 but not in any specific order.

6.1.15 Given code of Test.java file:

```java
package com.udayan.stream;

import java.util.stream.IntStream;

public class Test {
    public static void main(String[] args) {
        IntStream.rangeClosed(1, 10).parallel()
            .forEachOrdered(System.out::println);
    }
}
```

What will be the result of compiling and executing Test class?

A. It will print numbers from 1 to 10 in ascending order.

B. It will print numbers form 1 to 10 in descending order.

C. It will print numbers form 1 to 10 but not in any specific order.

6.1.16 Given code of Test.java file:

```java
package com.udayan.stream;

import java.util.stream.IntStream;

public class Test {
    public static void main(String[] args) {
        int res = IntStream.rangeClosed(1, 1000).parallel()
            .filter( i -> i > 50).findFirst().getAsInt();
        System.out.println(res);
    }
}
```

What will be the result of compiling and executing Test class?

A. It will always print 51.
B. It will print any number between 51 and 1000.
C. It will always print 50.
D. It will print any number between 1 and 50.

6.1.17 Can all streams be converted to parallel stream?

A. Yes
B. No

6.1.18 Performance with parallel stream is always better than sequential streams.

A. true
B. false

6.1.19 Given code of Test.java file:

```java
package com.udayan.stream;

import java.util.Arrays;
import java.util.List;

public class Test {
    private static StringBuilder RES = new StringBuilder();

    public static void main(String[] args) {
        List<String> list = Arrays.asList("A", "B", "C",
                    "D", "E", "F", "G", "H", "I", "J");
        list.parallelStream().forEach(RES::append);
        System.out.println(RES);
    }
}
```

What will be the result of compiling and executing Test class?

A. It will always print ABCDEFGHIJ.
B. Output cannot be predicted.
C. Compilation error.

6.1.20 Given code of Test.java file:

```
package com.udayan.stream;

import java.util.Arrays;
import java.util.List;

public class Test {
    public static void main(String[] args) {
        List<String> list =
            Arrays.asList("A", "E", "I", "O", "U");
        System.out.println(
            list._____.isParallel());
    }
}
```

Which of the options correctly fills the blank, such that output is true? Select ALL that apply.

A. stream().parallel()
B. stream()
C. parallel()
D. parallelStream()

6.1.21 Given code of Test.java file:

```java
package com.udayan.stream;

import java.util.stream.IntStream;

public class Test {
    public static void main(String[] args) {
        IntStream stream = IntStream.rangeClosed(1, 5);
        System.out.println(stream.parallel()
                .reduce((x, y) -> x + y).getAsInt());
    }
}
```

What will be the result of compiling and executing Test class?

A. It will print 15 on to the console.

B. It can print any number between 1 and 15.

C. It will print 0 on to the console.

D. None of the other options.

6.1.22 Given code of Test.java file:

```java
package com.udayan.stream;

import java.util.ArrayList;
import java.util.Collections;
import java.util.List;
import java.util.stream.IntStream;

public class Test {
    public static void main(String[] args) {
        List<Integer> list = Collections
                .synchronizedList(new ArrayList<>());
        IntStream stream = IntStream.rangeClosed(1, 7);
        stream.parallel().map(x -> {
            list.add(x); //Line 13
            return x;
        }).forEach(System.out::print); //Line 15
        System.out.println();
        list.forEach(System.out::print); //Line 17
    }
}
```

Which of the following statement is true about above code?

A. Line 15 and Line 17 will print exact same output on to the console.

B. Line 15 and Line 17 will not print exact same output on to the console.

C. Output cannot be predicted.

6.1.23 Given code of Test.java file:

```java
package com.udayan.stream;

import java.util.ArrayList;
import java.util.Collections;
import java.util.List;
import java.util.stream.IntStream;

public class Test {
    public static void main(String[] args) {
        List<Integer> list = Collections
                .synchronizedList(new ArrayList<>());
        IntStream stream = IntStream.rangeClosed(1, 7);
        stream.parallel().map(x -> {
            list.add(x); //Line 13
            return x;
        }).forEachOrdered(System.out::print); //Line 15
        System.out.println();
        list.forEach(System.out::print); //Line 17
    }
}
```

Which of the following statement is true about above code?

A. Line 15 and Line 17 will print exact same output on to the console.

B. Line 15 and Line 17 will not print exact same output on to the console.

C. Output of Line 15 can be predicted.

D. Output of Line 17 can be predicted.

E. Output of both Line 15 and Line 17 can be predicted.

6.1.24 Given code of Test.java file:

```java
package com.udayan.stream;

import java.util.Arrays;

public class Test {
    public static void main(String[] args) {
        String s1 = Arrays.asList("A", "E", "I", "O", "U")
            .stream().reduce("_", String::concat);
        String s2 = Arrays.asList("A", "E", "I", "O", "U")
            .parallelStream().reduce("_", String::concat);
        System.out.println(s1.equals(s2));
    }
}
```

What will be the result of compiling and executing Test class?

A. It will always print true.
B. It will always print false.
C. Output cannot be predicted.

6.1.25 Given code of Test.java file:

```java
package com.udayan.stream;

import java.util.Arrays;

public class Test {
    public static void main(String[] args) {
        String s1 = Arrays.asList("A", "E", "I", "O", "U")
            .stream().reduce("", String::concat);
        String s2 = Arrays.asList("A", "E", "I", "O", "U")
            .parallelStream().reduce("", String::concat);
        System.out.println(s1.equals(s2));
    }
}
```

What will be the result of compiling and executing Test class?

A. It will always print true.
B. It will always print false.
C. Output cannot be predicted.

6.1.26 Given code of Test.java file:

```java
package com.udayan.stream;

import java.util.stream.Stream;

public class Test {
    public static void main(String[] args) {
        String str1 =
            Stream.iterate(1, i -> i + 1).limit(10)
                .reduce("", (i, s) -> i + s,
                            (s1, s2) -> s1 + s2);
        String str2 =
            Stream.iterate(1, i -> i + 1).limit(10)
                .parallel()
                .reduce("", (i, s) -> i + s,
                            (s1, s2) -> s1 + s2);
        System.out.println(str1.equals(str2));
    }
}
```

What will be the result of compiling and executing Test class?

A. It will always print true.
B. It will always print false.
C. Output cannot be predicted.

6.1.27 Given code of Test.java file:

```java
package com.udayan.stream;

import java.util.stream.Stream;

public class Test {
    public static void main(String[] args) {
        Stream<String> stream =
            Stream.of("J", "A", "V", "A");
        String text = stream.parallel()
                    .reduce(String::concat).get();
        System.out.println(text);
    }
}
```

What will be the result of compiling and executing Test class?

A. It will always print JAVA on to the console.

B. Output cannot be predicted.

C. None of the other options.

6.2 Answers of Practice Test - 6 with Explanation

6.1.1 Answer: B, D

Reason:
Iterator<T> interface has forEach(Consumer) method. As Consumer is a Functional Interface, hence a lambda expression or method reference syntax can be passed as argument to forEach() method.

list.forEach(System.out::print); => This will print 100020003000 without any newline character in between.
list.forEach(System.out::println); => This prints desired output
list.forEach(i -> System.out.println(i)); => Causes compilation failure as lambda expression variable 'i' conflicts with local variable.
list.forEach(s -> System.out.println(s)); => Prints desired output.

NOTE: 'System.out::print' is a method reference syntax corresponding to lambda expression 's -> System.out.println(s)'.

6.1.2 Answer: A

Reason:
Iterator<T> interface has forEach(Consumer) method. As Consumer is a Functional Interface and it has 'void accept(T t)' method, hence a lambda expression for 1 parameter can be passed as argument to forEach(...) method.

'e -> e.setSalary(e.getSalary() + (e.getSalary() * .2))' => increments the salary of all the employees by 20%.
'System.out::println' => prints employee object on to the console.

As salary is of double type, so decimal point (.) is shown in the output.

6.1.3   Answer: C

Reason:
Arrays class has overloaded stream(...) method to convert arrays to Stream.
sorted(...) method of Stream interface is also overloaded: sorted() => sorts on natural order and sorted(Comparator) => sorts on passed Comparator.

sorted((s1,s2) -> s2.compareTo(s1)) => sorts on descending order.

forEach(System.out::println); => Prints all the Stream data.

6.1.4   Answer: B

Reason:
Interface Collection has stream() method which returns sequential stream and parallelStream() method with returns parallel stream.
In this case, list.stream() returns a sequential stream.

Uppercase characters are different from Lowercase characters.
distinct() method of Stream returns a stream consisting of the distinct elements (according to Object.equals(Object)) of this stream.

"A" and "A" are same, "b" and "B" are different & "c" and "c" are same.

Arrays.asList(...) method returns sequential List object, so order of elements remain same.

Output is: AbBc

6.1.5   Answer: B

Reason:
Streams are lazily evaluated, which means if terminal operations such as: forEach, count, toArray, reduce, collect, findFirst, findAny, anyMatch, allMatch, sum, min, max, average etc. are not present, the given stream pipeline is not evaluated and hence map() method doesn't reverse the stream elements.

'[abc, xyz]' is printed on to the console.

If you replace 'list.stream().map(x -> x.reverse());' with 'list.stream().map(x -> x.reverse()).count();' then output will be: '[cba, zyx]'.

6.1.6   Answer: C

Reason:
chars() method in String class returns IntStream, all the elements in this stream are stored as int value of corresponding char.

filter(Test::isDirection) => Returns the stream consisting of int (char) for which isDirection method returns true. isDirection method returns true for 'N', 'E', 'W' and 'S' only, for other characters (including whitespace character) it returns false.

forEach(c -> System.out.print((char)c)); => forEach method typecast int value to char and hence NEWS is printed on to the console.

6.1.7   Answer: C

Reason:
Arrays.asList(...) method returns a list backed with array, so items cannot be added to or removed from the list.

But if this list is passed to the constructor of ArrayList, then new ArrayList instance is created which copies the elements of passed list and elements can be added to or removed from this list.

List<Integer> list = new ArrayList<>(Arrays.asList(1,2,3,4,5,6,7,8,9,10)); => [1,2,3,4,5,6,7,8,9,10].
Default method removeIf was added in Collection interface and it accepts a Predicate. It removes all the elements for which passed Predicate is true.

In the given case, list.removeIf(i -> i % 2 == 1); => [2,4,6,8,10].

6.1.8 Answer: C

Reason:
stream.collect(Collectors.toList()) returns an instance of ArrayList and hence output will always be in ascending order as stream was sorted using sorted() method before converting to list.

6.1.9 Answer: C

Reason:
Set doesn't allow duplicates, which means generated set will have 4 elements ["java", "python", "c", "c++"] and therefore set.size() will return 4.

6.1.10 Answer: A

Reason:
'TreeSet::new' is same as '() -> new TreeSet()'

TreeSet contains unique elements and in sorted order, in this case natural order.

Output will always be: [c, c++, java, python]

6.1.11 Answer: D

Reason:
Variable id has package scope and as class Test is in the same package hence p.id doesn't cause any compilation error.

'Collectors.toMap(p -> p.id, Function.identity())' and 'Collectors.toMap(p -> p.id, p -> p)' are exactly same as 'Function.identity()' is same as lambda expression 'p -> p'.

Collectors.toCollection(TreeMap::new) causes compilation error as TreeMap doesn't extend from Collection interface.

6.1.12 Answer: B

Reason:
Rest of the code is very simple, let us concentrate on partitioning code.

Collectors.partitioningBy(s -> s.equals("OCA")) => s in this lambda expression is of Certification type and not String type.
This means predicate 's -> s.equals("OCA")' will return false for "OCA". None of the certification object will return true and hence no element will be stored against 'true'.

[] will be printed in the output.

Correct predicate will be: 's -> s.getTest().equals("OCA")'.

For above predicate, output for 'System.out.println(map.get(true));' will be:
[{S001, OCA, 87}, {S002, OCA, 82}, {S003, OCA, 60}, {S004, OCA, 88}]

6.1.13 Answer: D

Reason:
Collectors.groupingBy(Certification::getTest) => groups on the basis of test which is String type. Hence return type is: Map<String, List<Certification>>.

There are 4 records for OCA exam and 2 records for OCP exam, hence map.get("OCP") returns the list containing OCP records.

6.1.14 Answer: C

Reason:
IntStream.rangeClosed(1, 10) returns a sequential ordered IntStream but parallel() method converts it to a parallel stream. Hence, forEach method doesn't guarantee the order for printing numbers.

6.1.15   Answer: A

Reason:
IntStream.rangeClosed(1, 10) returns a sequential ordered IntStream but parallel() method converts it to a parallel stream.
forEachOrdered() will processes the elements of the stream in the order specified by its source (Encounter order), regardless of whether the stream is sequential or parallel, hence given code prints 1 to 10 in ascending order.

6.1.16   Answer: A

Reason:
First element that matches the filter is 51.
In this case, base stream is sequential ordered IntStream (it has specific Encounter Order), hence findFirst() method will always return 51 regardless of whether the stream is sequential or parallel.

6.1.17   Answer: A

Reason:
All streams in Java implements BaseStream interface and this interface has parallel() and sequential() methods. Hence all streams can either be parallel or sequential.

6.1.18   Answer: B

Reason:
Parallel streams internally use fork/join framework only, so there is always an overhead of splitting the tasks and joining the results.

Parallel streams improves performance for streams with large number of elements, easily splittable into independent operations and computations are complex.

6.1.19 Answer: B

Reason:
list.parallelStream() returns a parallel stream.

Method reference 'RES::append' is same as lambda expression 's -> RES.append(s)'.
NOTE: In the lambda expression as static variable RES is used hence given code suffers from race condition.

Output cannot be predicted in this case.

6.1.20 Answer: A,D

Reason:
Collection interface has a default method stream() to return a sequential() stream for the currently executing Collection.
Collection interface has a default method parallelStream() to return a parallel stream for the currently executing Collection.

Stream class has parallel() method to convert to parallel stream and sequential() method to convert to sequential stream.
isParallel() method of Stream class returns true for parallel Stream.

list is a Collection. So,

list.stream() returns a sequential stream and list.stream().parallel() returns a parallel stream. list.stream().parallel().isParallel() returns true.
stream() returns a sequential stream and list.stream().isParallel() returns false.
list.parallel() causes compilation error.
list.parallelStream() returns a parallel stream. list.parallelStream().isParallel() returns true.

6.1.21 Answer: A

Reason:
stream --> {1, 2, 3, 4, 5}.
stream.parallel() returns a parallel stream.

To understand, 'reduce((x, y) -> x + y)' is equivalent to:

```
boolean foundAny = false;
int result = null;
for (int element : this stream) {
 if (!foundAny) {
    foundAny = true;
    result = element;
 }
 else
    result = accumulator.applyAsInt(result, element);
}
return foundAny ? OptionalInt.of(result) : OptionalInt.empty();
```

result will be initialized to 1st element of the stream and output will be the result of '1 + 2 + 3 + 4 + 5', which is 15.

The whole computation may run in parallel, but parallelism doesn't impact final result. In this case as there are only 5 numbers, hence it is an overhead to use parallelism.

reduce((x, y) -> x + y) returns OptionalInt and it has getAsInt() method.

6.1.22 Answer: C

Reason:
Line 13 is changing the state of list object and hence it should be avoided in parallel stream. You can never predict the order in which elements will be added to the stream.

Line 13 and Line 15 doesn't run in synchronized manner, hence as the result, output of Line 17 may be different from that of Line 15.

On my machine below is the output of various executions:
Execution 1:
5427163
5412736

Execution 2:
5476231
5476123

Execution 3:
5476231
5476231

6.1.23 Answer: C

Reason:
Line 13 is changing the state of list object and hence it should be avoided in parallel stream. You can never predict the order in which elements will be added to the stream.

Line 13 and Line 15 doesn't run in synchronized manner, hence as the result, output of Line 17 may be different from that of Line 15.

forEachOrdered() will processes the elements of the stream in the order specified by its source, regardless of whether the stream is sequential or parallel.

As forEachOrdered() method is used at Line 15, hence Line 15 will always print '1234567' on to the console.

On my machine below is the output of various executions:
Execution 1:
1234567
1352764

Execution 2:
1234567
6514327

Execution 3:
1234567
1732645

6.1.24 Answer: C

Reason:
reduce method in Stream class is declared as: T reduce(T identity, BinaryOperator<T> accumulator)
By checking the reduce method, 'reduce("", String::concat)', we can say that:
Identity is String type, accumulator is BinaryOperator<String> type.

Though you may always get false but result cannot be predicted as identity value ("_") used in reduce method is not following an important rule.

For each element 't' of the stream, accumulator.apply(identity, t) is equal to t.

'String::concat' is equivalent to lambda expression '(s1, s2) -> s1.concat(s2);'.

For 1st element of the stream, "A" accumulator.apply("_", "A") results in "_A", which is not equal to "A" and hence rule is not followed.

s1 will always refer to "_AEIOU" but s2 may refer to various possible string objects depending upon how parallel stream is processed.

s2 may refer to "_A_E_I_O_U" or "_AE_I_OU" or "_AEIOU". So output cannot be predicted.

6.1.25 Answer: A

Reason:
reduce method in Stream class is declared as: T reduce(T identity, BinaryOperator<T> accumulator)
By checking the reduce method, 'reduce("", String::concat)', we can say that:
Identity is String type, accumulator is BinaryOperator<String> type.

'String::concat' is equivalent to lambda expression '(s1, s2) -> s1.concat(s2);'.

To get consistent output, there are requirements for reduce method arguments:
1. For each element 't' of the stream, accumulator.apply(identity, t) is equal to t.
   For 1st element of the stream, "A" accumulator.apply("", "A") results in "A", which is equal to "A" and hence 1st rule is followed.

2. The accumulator operator (concat) in this case must be associative and stateless.
   concat is associative as (s1.concat(s2)).concat(s3) equals to s1.concat(s2.concat(s3)).
   Given method reference syntax is stateless as well.

As both the rules are followed, hence reduce will give the same result for both sequential and parallel stream.

6.1.26 Answer: A

Reason:
reduce method in Stream class is declared as: <U> U reduce(U identity, BiFunction<U,? super T,U> accumulator, BinaryOperator<U> combiner)
By checking the reduce method 'reduce("", (i, s) -> i + s, (s1, s2) -> s1 + s2)', we can say that:
Identity is String type, accumulator is BiFunction<String, ? super Integer, String> type, combiner is BinaryOperator<String> type.

To get consistent output, there are requirements for reduce method arguments:
1. The identity value must be an identity for the combiner function. This means that for all u, combiner(identity, u) is equal to u.
   As u is of String type, let's say u = "X", combiner("", "X") = "X". Hence, u is equal to combiner("", "X"). First rule is obeyed.

2. The combiner function must be compatible with the accumulator function; for all u and t, the following must hold:
   combiner.apply(u, accumulator.apply(identity, t)) == accumulator.apply(u, t).
   Let's consider, u = "Y", t is element of Stream, say t = 1, identity = "".
   combiner.apply(u, accumulator.apply(identity, t))
   = combiner.apply("Y", accumulator.apply("", 1))
   = combiner.apply("Y", "1")
   = "Y1"

   and

   accumulator.apply(u, t)
   = accumulator.apply("Y", 1)
   = "Y1"

Hence, combiner.apply(u, accumulator.apply(identity, t)) == accumulator.apply(u, t). 2nd rule is also followed.

3. The accumulator operator must be associative and stateless. Operator + is associative and lambda expression is stateless. 3rd rule is followed.

4. The combiner operator must be associative and stateless. Operator + is associative and lambda expression is stateless. 4th rule is followed.

As all the rules are followed in this case, hence str1 refers to "12345678910" and str2 refers to "12345678910"

6.1.27 Answer: A

Reason:

reduce method in Stream class is declared as: 'Optional<T> reduce(BinaryOperator<T> accumulator);'

'String::concat' is equivalent to lambda expression '(s1, s2) -> s1.concat(s2);'.
By checking the reduce method, 'reduce(String::concat)' we can say that:
accumulator is BinaryOperator<String> type.

To get consistent output, accumulator must be associative and stateless. concat is associative as (s1.concat(s2)).concat(s3) equals to s1.concat(s2.concat(s3)). Given method reference syntax is stateless as well.

Hence, reduce will give the same result for both sequential and parallel stream.

As per Javadoc, given reduce method is equivalent to:

boolean foundAny = false;
T result = null;
for (T element : this stream) {
 if (!foundAny) {
    foundAny = true;
    result = element;
 }
 else
    result = accumulator.apply(result, element);
}
return foundAny ? Optional.of(result) : Optional.empty();

This means, output will be JAVA.

Printed in Great Britain
by Amazon